A JOURNEY THROUGH THE BIBLE

A JOURNEY THROUGH THE BIBLE

Volume 4
1 Timothy to Revelation

DENIS LYLE

Christian Year Publications

ISBN-13: 978 1 912522 85 9

Typeset by John Ritchie Ltd., Kilmarnock
Printed by Bell & Bain Ltd., Glasgow

"But continue thou in the things which thou hast learned and hast been assured of, knowing of whom thou hast learned them; And that from a child thou hast known the holy scriptures, which are able to make thee wise unto salvation through faith which is in Christ Jesus. All scripture is given by inspiration of God, and is profitable for doctrine, for reproof, for correction, for instruction in righteousness: That the man of God may be perfect, thoroughly furnished unto all good works."

2 Timothy 3:14-17

Contents

Endorsement

It was my privilege to serve with Denis on the oversight of Lurgan Baptist Church during his period as pastor there which commmenced in March 1998 and lasted for almost twenty years.

One of the things which impressed me about all his pulpit ministry was the amount of work that went into his preparation. It was always evident and is clearly seen in these books.

It was especially evident in the Bible Class and the number of people who attended from other churches was testimony to the help they obtained from his Bible exposition.

I heard these messages preached week by week as he took us through the entire Bible and I recall suggesting to him towards the end of the series that it would be profitable if the series could be produced in book form.

My feeling then was that it would be a useful tool for anyone wanting to study a book of the Bible as it would give an overview which could be used as a starting point to lead into the book.

The content of these books goes far beyond that. If, for example, you look at any chapter, you will see that you not only have the overview but also a concise summary of the sections of the book and the doctrines taught in each.

I heartily commend these books to you. They will be a help to all who read their Bible.

Denis, we owe you a debt of gratitude for all that has gone into this series. May God bless you and continue to use you in His work.

Walton Gracey
Former elder, Lurgan Baptist Church.

Foreword

It was in July 2016 that I first met Denis. I had benefitted from the oral and written material on his website: *unsearchableriches. org.* and, while in Newcastle, Northern Ireland for the Northfield Bible Weeks, I made contact with him. We met for coffee and had a lovely conversation together. The result has been the very pleasant task of converting some of his sermons into books.

I vividly remember being moved to tears while reading his draft transcript of *"From Earth to Glory"*. His thoughts on Psalm 23 were very comforting indeed – and that book, published to coincide with his final Bible Class at Lurgan Baptist Church in March 2017, has been such a blessing to many as they have faced the trials of life.

From the autumn of 2013 until the spring of 2017, Denis took his Bible Class on: "A Journey Through the Bible". The messages he preached have now become a four-volume series. Volume 1, covering Genesis to Esther, was published in August 2017 and this was followed in July 2018 by Volume 2 which dealt with Job to Malachi. Volume 3 – Matthew to 2 Thessalonians – appeared in July 2019, and this Volume brings the series to an end.

Each book of the Bible is examined in a chapter of approximately twenty pages with a combination of appropriate anecdotes, interesting information, helpful headings and excellent exposition. (Denis and I share a love for alliteration!)

I am aware how much effort Denis put in while preparing for each meeting – hours and hours, sometimes days and days, of study, but that labour was not in vain. Substantial numbers of Christians, with some travelling quite a distance, gathered Tuesday by

Tuesday to hear Denis preach. They were helped spiritually – and that beneficial effect has continued with the publication of these books. The feedback regarding the first three Volumes has been very positive indeed.

On 1st September 2017, as a family we attended the Farewell Service for Denis as he stepped down as pastor at Lurgan. Hundreds gathered and the tributes given were heart-felt. It was obvious that those among whom he had served esteemed him very highly. He loved them and they loved him. Denis' sphere of ministry has subsequently changed. He is now able to travel widely across Northern Ireland and further afield – and increasing numbers of Christians are able to sit under his preaching and teaching. It has been a privilege for me to be able to introduce others to Denis through this series of books.

The friendship with Denis that commenced at that first meeting in July 2016 has continued and deepened since then. He and I are in touch frequently and often have long conversations together. I am honoured to be able to regard him now as a dear friend. He and his wife Catherine have extended hospitality to us as a family – and this has been much appreciated. In September 2019, Denis officiated at my son Jonathan's wedding and I know that Jonathan and Brianna both valued the very powerful wedding sermon he preached.

Looking back over my life as a Christian, perhaps the Bible teacher who taught me most was the late Willie Mullan. Back in the 1980s, I discovered his preaching. Listening to numerous recordings on a variety of subjects, I was greatly helped. Little did I think then that in subsequent years I would have such a close relationship with one of his successors.

Denis, I am so grateful to the Lord for allowing our paths to cross. I am indebted to you for so much. May the Master be pleased to continue to bless you in your service for Him.

Fraser A Munro
Windygates, Fife.

Preface

From the autumn of 2013 until the spring of 2017, I took those who attended the Tuesday night Bible Class at Lurgan Baptist Church on a Journey through the Bible. On this Journey, I took one book of the Bible each night and sought to give an overview of it.

Thanks to the willingness of John Ritchie Ltd, the Christian publishers, I have now been able to take readers on a similar Journey. Volume 1 appeared in August 2017 and this fourth Volume brings the series to a close.

It was a great encouragement to me to hear from many who listened to my teaching that they had been helped by the ministry. It has been an added encouragement to hear from those who have enjoyed reading these books.

As you read, you will see that I drew widely from all sorts of writers. Their books on the Bible enlightened me, enriched me and encouraged me and some of their content is found in these Volumes. That is my disclaimer to plagiarism.

As the series concludes, it would be appropriate for me to thank those who played a part in the production of these books. Irene Campbell transcribed my sermons for her own purposes – and her record has proved to be extremely useful. Bertie Campbell has been a very diligent proof-reader and I am grateful to him for all his work. Finally, I would like to thank Fraser Munro. Others had suggested to me that it would be good if my messages could be converted into books, but it was Fraser who was able to take the project forward. I appreciate the hours of work he has spent. These books could not have been published without his involvement.

I want also to thank my wife Catherine who has stood by me since we began **'our journey'** together for the Lord almost forty seven years ago. Above all, I want to thank the Lord for His saving grace and keeping power. I often ponder the words of Paul in 1 Corinthians 4 verse 7: *"What hast thou that thou didst not receive?"* All that I am, have and ever hope to be is from the Lord - and I am daily thankful to Him.

It is appropriate that I close this *Preface* to Volume 4 in the same way that I have closed each previous *Preface*: As you ponder the pages of *'A Journey Through the Bible'*, I trust that you will have a new appreciation of the written Word and a fresh appreciation of our wonderful Saviour, of whom this Book so eloquently speaks.

Denis Lyle
Moira
Northern Ireland
February 2020

Additional material from Denis Lyle can be read, heard and viewed on Denis' website: www.unsearchableriches.org.

Bibliography

Unlocking the Bible: J. David Pawson - Collins
Willmington's Guide to the Bible: H.L. Willmington - Tyndale House, Wheaton, Illinois
Wiersbe's Expository Outlines on the New Testament: Warren Wiersbe - Victor Books
The Bible Exposition Commentary: Warren Wiersbe - Victor Books
The Message of the Old Testament: Mark Dever - Crossway Books
The Message of the New Testament: Mark Dever - Crossway Books
The MacArthur Bible Handbook: John MacArthur - Thomas Nelson
Adventuring Through the Bible: Ray Stedman - Discovery House Publishers
God's Wonderful Word: Trevor Knight - Young Life
A Sure Foundation: Alan Cairns - Ambassador
Bible Survey Outlines: Roland V. Hudson - Eerdmans Publishing Company
Explore The Book: J. Sidlow Baxter - Zondervan Publishing House
The Bible Book by Book: Raymond Brown - Collins
Know your Bible: Graham Scroggie - Pickering & Inglis
From Cover to Cover: Brian Harbour - Broadman Press
Exploring the Old Testament Book by Book: John Phillips - Kregel
Exploring the New Testament Book by Book: John Phillips - Kregel
The Old Testament: Gareth Crossley - Evangelical Press
Jensen's Survey of the Old Testament: Irving Jensen - Moody Press
A Survey of the New Testament: Robert H. Gundry - The Paternoster Press
The Collected Writings of J.B. Hewitt: Gospel Tract Publications
Basic Bible Study Notes: Ian Brown (Martyrs Memorial Free Presbyterian Church, Belfast)
An Introduction to the New Testament: Lamoyne Sharpe - Printed in U.S.A.

1 Timothy

"Men wanted for hazardous journey. Small wages, bitter cold, long months of complete darkness, constant danger. Safe return doubtful. Honour and recognition in case of success."

The advertisement appeared in a London newspaper and thousands of men responded. It was signed by the noted Artic explorer Sir Ernest Shackleton - and that was what made the difference.

If the Lord Jesus had advertised for workers, the announcement might have read something like this:

"Men and women wanted for difficult task of helping to build My church. You will often be misunderstood, even by those working with you. You will face constant attack from an invisible enemy. You may not see the results of your labour and your full reward will not come till after all your work is completed. It may cost you your home, your ambition and even your life."

In spite of the demands the Lord makes, He receives *"the applications"* of many who gladly give their all for Him.

Timothy, whose name means: *"one who honours God"*, was one young man who responded to Christ's call to build His church.

Who was he? Timothy was probably from Lystra. He was the son of a Greek father and a Jewish mother Eunice (Acts 16:1-2 and 2 Timothy 1:5). He probably was saved at the age of fifteen or so during Paul's first missionary journey (Acts 14). His father seems to have died when Timothy was young, resulting in him being raised by his godly mother, Eunice, and his saintly grandmother, Lois. These two wonderful women instilled into the boy a good grounding in the things of God. *When Paul came back to Lystra on his second missionary journey Timothy was nearly twenty.* Even at this early age he was showing great potential for he *"was well reported of by the brethren that were at Lystra and Iconium"* (Acts 16:2). It was here that Timothy was added to Paul's missionary team. Timothy was to be Paul's disciple, friend and co-labourer for the rest of the apostle's life, ministering with him in Berea (Acts 17:14); Athens (Acts 17:15); Corinth (Acts 18:5 and 2 Corinthians 1:19) and accompanying him on his trip to Jerusalem (Acts 20:4). He was with Paul in his first Roman imprisonment and went to Philippi (Philippians 2:19-23) after Paul's release. When Paul was back in prison again for the last time, we find him urging Timothy, with deep emotion, to hurry to his side (2 Timothy 4:21).

Tradition tells us that Timothy lived until about 70 years of age and that he was martyred by the Ephesian idolaters for protesting against their licentiousness and idol worship.

So much for the man. What about this letter? Well, I want you to think about:

1. The Background to this Letter

The Book of Acts closes with Paul a prisoner in Rome. He was tried and acquitted, probably in A.D. 63. When the great fire of Rome broke out in A.D. 64, Paul was on a fourth missionary journey (A.D. 63-67) which took him to Philippi (Philippians 2:24); to Colosse (Philemon 22) and perhaps on to Spain (Romans 15:28). He then came back to Ephesus where he found that the heresies he had anticipated (Acts 20:28-30) had already taken root. Leaving Timothy behind to deal with the problems that had arisen, Paul went on to Macedonia from where he wrote Timothy this letter to help him carry out his task in the church (1 Timothy 3:14-15).

Then there is:

2. The Burden of this Letter

What is Paul's burden as he writes to his *"son in the faith"*?

Here is a young pastor/teacher facing many difficult problems in a *"big city church"*. Timothy was a young man seeking to pastor older people (1 Timothy 4:12 and Chapter 5:1-2) and this was not an easy thing to do. Timothy greatly missed Paul and wanted to quit (1 Timothy 1:3 and 2 Timothy 1:4). Timothy was prone to neglect his pastoral duties and his devotional life as a Christian leader (1 Timothy 4:11-16).

So, keeping this all in mind, what was Paul's burden for Timothy and the church? Well, the basic theme of the book is summarized in 1 Timothy 3:15:

"That thou mayest know how thou oughtest to behave thyself in the house of God, which is the church of the living God, the pillar and ground of the truth."

Here is Paul's reason for writing to Timothy.

The church is the pillar and ground of the truth. Paul's imagery may have referred to the magnificent temple of Diana (also known as Artemis) in Ephesus which was supported by 127 gold-plated marble pillars. The word translated: *"ground"* appears only here in the New Testament and denotes the foundation on which a building rests. You see, here is the function of the church. The church upholds the truth of God's revealed Word. The *"truth"* is the content of the Christian faith recorded in Scripture and is summed up in verse 16:

"And without controversy great is the mystery of godliness: God was manifest in the flesh, justified in the Spirit, seen of angels, preached unto the Gentiles, believed on in the world, received up into glory."

Have we grasped this clearly? Alan Cairns in his book, *"A Sure Foundation"*, states:

"The church of God in this world is the upholder of the truth. That is the basic function of every true church of Jesus Christ. There are many important tasks for the church to perform, but everything else is subservient to her fundamental responsibility to uphold the truth of God in Christ. How may we recognize a true church? A true church of Christ upholds the truth of God."

That is the burden of Paul for Timothy and the Ephesians.

3. The Benefits of this Letter

Along with 2 Timothy and Titus, these letters are known as *"the pastoral epistles"*. No doubt they contain much information that is helpful for pastors, but they also focus on the need for elders and deacons. They expect a number of men to be appointed as elders. Moreover, in this book Paul deals with the role of women in the church.

He talks about members, ministers and money.

So the benefits of this book are numerous. I have divided it into five sections:

(1) DOCTRINE DEFENDED
Chapter 1

Keep in mind that as Paul writes to Timothy he is aware of the problems he faces in the church.

> Paul is awake to the perils.
> Paul is alive to the possibilities.
> Paul is alert to the privileges.

Paul is now advising Timothy in the position he is taking over.

The first thing that he deals with is doctrine. Now everything has its foundation here. If truth is missing, if the teaching is wrong, all is wrong.

The Bible is a book of doctrine. Do you see how Paul describes it in verse 10 of this chapter? *"Sound doctrine."* The expression literally means: *"healthy teaching"*, that is, teaching that promotes spiritual health. Our word: *"hygiene"* comes from this Greek word. It is used again in 2 Timothy 1 verse 13, 2 Timothy 4 verse 3 and Titus 1 verses 9 and 13 and Chapter 2 verses 1, 2 and 8.

So Paul begins here with doctrine. Indeed, he says to Timothy: *"O Timothy, keep that which is committed to thy trust"* (1 Timothy 6:20). The word: *"keep"* means: *"guard"*. The expression: *"that which is committed to thy trust"* is a single word that simply means: *"the deposit"*. What is Timothy's responsibility? *"To guard the deposit"* that God had committed to him through Paul. What is the deposit? Well, look at verse 11 of Chapter 1: *"the glorious gospel of the blessed God, which was committed to my trust"* or: *"the glad tidings of the glory of the blessed God with which I was entrusted"*. Paul then proceeds to expound the leading truths of this gospel in 1 Timothy 1 verse 15, then in Chapter 2 verses 5 and 6 and then in Chapter 3 verse 16.

God had given the gospel message, the deposit of truth, to Paul (1 Timothy 1:11), who had in turn committed it to Timothy (1 Timothy 1:18-19). Timothy was to guard it and pass it on to others (2 Timothy 2:2).

Is this not the task of the church today?

Paul begins by defending doctrine. Notice there was:

(a) THE PERVERSION OF SOUND DOCTRINE:
Chapter 1 verses 1-4

Look at verses 3 and 4:

"As I besought thee to abide still at Ephesus, when I went into Macedonia, that thou mightest charge some that they teach no other doctrine, Neither give heed to fables and endless genealogies, which minister questions, rather than godly edifying which is in faith: so do."

Do you recall what Paul said when he was saying: *"Farewell!"* to the elders of Ephesus?

He said:

"Wherefore I take you to record this day, that I am pure from the blood of all men. For I have not shunned to declare unto you all the counsel of God. Take heed therefore unto yourselves, and to all the flock, over the which the Holy Ghost hath made you overseers" (Acts 20:26-28).

A Bible College does not make a pastor or an elder. Nor is it done through the vote of a church. This is the work of the Holy Ghost.

Why were overseers appointed?

Acts 20 verse 28 continues and provides the answer: *"to feed the church of God, which He hath purchased with His own blood"*.

Paul warns these overseers.

There is going to be Danger from Without

"For I know this, that after my departing shall grievous wolves enter in among you, not sparing the flock" (Acts 20:29).

There is going to be Danger from Within

"Also of your own selves shall men arise, speaking perverse things, to draw away disciples after them" (Acts 20:30).

Some Bible scholars believe that the false teachers were elders (1 Timothy 1:7, Chapter 3:2 and Chapter 5:17), perhaps Hymenaeus and Alexander (1 Timothy 1:19-20). Be that as it may, Paul identified this false teaching as *"fables and endless genealogies"*. These false teachers were using the Old Testament law and especially the genealogies to manufacture all kinds of novelties. These new doctrines were leading people astray.

Do you see that phrase in verse 4: *"Rather than godly edifying"*? We could translate it: *"Rather than God's saving plan which is by faith"*.

Whatever this heresy was (whether Jewish legalism, Gnosticism or a mixture of both), it struck a blow at the gospel of saving faith. You see, all the belief systems of the world fall into two classes.

There is the gospel of divine accomplishment, that Christ accomplished salvation apart from human effort.
There is the religion of human achievement where men attempt to gain salvation by their own works.

It seems that these false teachers at Ephesus offered a way to God which required human achievement.

Paul was having none of it!

"Charge some that they teach no other doctrine."

Is this not our responsibility? To warn people against *"things contrary to sound doctrine"*. To lift up the standard of God's Word. To oppose the encroachments of error. To recognise false doctrine. To reprove false teachers. Indeed, to receive them not (2 John 10).

(b) THE PURITY OF SOUND DOCTRINE
Chapter 1 verses 5-12

Paul refers to doctrine in 1 Timothy 6 verse 3 as: *"the doctrine which is according to godliness"*. Sound doctrine leads to sound living which is godliness. In the church at Ephesus, where Timothy was ministering, certain people were spreading teaching of their own that was contrary to Scripture. Instead of producing love, purity, a good conscience and sincere faith, these novel doctrines were causing division, hypocrisy and all sorts of problems. It seems that some were trying to control the conduct of the Christians through regulations, that is legalism. But Paul says the law is made for the unrighteous not the righteous.

The lawful use of the law is to expose, restrain and convict the lawless. The law cannot save lost sinners. It can only reveal their need for a Saviour.

When a sinner trusts Christ, he is freed from the curse of the law (Galatians 3:10-14) and the righteous demands of the law are met by the indwelling Spirit as the believer yields to the Lord (Romans 8:1-4).

Do we not need to listen carefully to ensure that what is said is Scriptural? To ensure that what is sung is Scriptural? Far too many songs either teach no doctrine or teach false doctrine. A singer has no more right to sing a lie than a teacher has to teach a lie!

(c) THE POWER OF SOUND DOCTRINE
Chapter 1 verses 12-17

It is the *"glorious gospel"* (1 Timothy 1:11) that saves lost sinners. Paul had experienced the power of the gospel and had been entrusted with the ministry of the gospel.

Timothy was disturbed because he thought he was too young and lacked the necessary qualifications for ministry.

"Look at me", says Paul. *"I was a blasphemer and a murderer before God saved me. If the grace of God can make a missionary out of a murderer then it can make a success of you!"*

Are you perhaps despairing of your unsaved family? Do you think they are too hard for the Lord? Well, do you see what Paul says here? He says his conversion is *"a pattern"* (verse 16). It is just an example of what God can do for lost sinners. Here is a conversion that is a picture of all conversions. We see here that no man or woman is too bad for the redeeming grace of God to transform. No wonder Paul bursts forth into song:

"Now unto the King eternal, immortal, invisible, the only wise God, be honour and glory for ever and ever. Amen."

Paul concludes this section with:

(d) THE PERSEVERANCE OF SOUND DOCTRINE
Chapter 1 verses 18-20

Paul charges Timothy. He reminds him that God has chosen him for ministry. Some in the local church had been instructed to single Timothy out and ordain him for special service (1 Timothy 4:14 and 2 Timothy 1:6). Paul is saying: *"Timothy, God has equipped you for battle!"*

Like Timothy, do you want to resign? Almost every Christian worker at one time or another has wanted to quit, but as Dr. Raymond Edman, former president of Wheaton College, used to say: *"It is always too soon to quit"*.

Paul says: *"Timothy! Labour in the word and doctrine"*. The word: *"labour"* means: *"work at it"*.

In an age when many say: *"It does not matter what you believe"*, God says: *"Study sound doctrine; stress sound doctrine; support sound doctrine and stand for sound doctrine"*.

(2) DEVOTION DESCRIBED
Chapter 2

Paul turns from *the church and its doctrine* to *the church and its devotions*. He has now some things to say about prayer, preaching and position within the church. Notice that he deals here with:

(a) The Practice of Worship in the Church
Chapter 2 verses 1-8

In Chapter 1, Paul's emphasis is on the *Word*. In Chapter 2, his emphasis is on *prayer*. You see, the two main ministries of the pastor/teacher are the Word of God and prayer.

Warren Wiersbe says:

"It is sad to see churches robbing their pastors of these important ministries by keeping them busy promoting a program, pleasing people and practising church politics. If the churches would simplify their organization and purify their motives the pastors would be able to do a spiritual work for the glory of the Lord."

Do you recall the desire of the apostles in Acts 6 verse 4? *"But we will give ourselves continually to prayer, and to the ministry of the Word."*

> The Word enlightens us, prayer enables us.
> The Word instructs us, prayer inspires us.
> The Word brings light, prayer brings heat.

There is to be this balanced ministry of the Word of God and prayer.

Can you see here:

The *Why* of Prayer:

"First of all." That indicates priority. One pastor said: *"If I announce a banquet, a dinner, people will come out of the woodwork to attend, but if I announce a prayer meeting, I am fortunate if the ushers show up!"*

God wants us to pray for our praying has an effect nationally (verse 2) and spiritually (verse 4).

The *What* of Prayer:

"Supplications" - those are requests.

"Prayers" - a general term suggesting reverence.

"Intercessions" - suggests petitions.

"Giving of thanks"- for who God is and for what He does for us.

The *Who* of Prayer:

"For Kings" – and remember that the godless Nero was on the throne at this time, the very man who would order Paul's death.

"For all that are in authority" - for the government and its members.

"For all men" - (1 Timothy 2:4-7). We need to pray for the salvation of all men on the basis of the work of Jesus Christ.

The *How* of Prayer:

It is to be *Without Delay!* *"I will therefore that men pray"*
It is to be *Without Defilement!* *"Holy hands"*
It is to be *Without Discord!* *"Without wrath"*
It is to be *Without Doubting!* *"Without wrath and doubting"*

Much prayer: much power.
No prayer: no power.

(b) The Place of Women in the Church
Chapter 2 verses 9-15

The Christian faith like no other elevated the position of women and children. Instead of criticising Paul for these instructions given by him about women, women ought to thank God for the blessing the Christian faith has been to women around the world.

But, no, Paul's teaching has been rejected out of hand by modern feminists. They say: *"Paul was a crusty old bachelor"*. They accuse him of being anti-women.

Perhaps we need to keep in mind the three-fold headship in the local assembly.

1. The Headship of Christ over the body (Colossians 1:18).
2. The Headship of the Elders over the flock (Acts 20:28).
3. The Headship of the Man over the woman (1 Corinthians 11:1-16).

Now keeping that in mind Paul says that the ladies are to be marked *by Modesty.* Do not major on the external but the internal. Now, this does not mean that a woman should neglect herself. Some women think it is a mark of spirituality to look like an unmade bed! Vance Havner once said: *"To be all out for God, you don't have to look all in!"* Christian women can dress smartly and modestly with an outfit that does not accentuate the precise shape of her body. She can dress distinctly so as to maintain the distinction of the sexes. But remember, external beauty is passing, internal beauty is permanent. The former is attractive to the world, the latter is pleasing to God.

She is to be marked *by Humility*. Do you see verses 11 and 12?

"Let the woman learn in silence with all subjection. But I suffer not a woman to teach, nor to usurp authority over the man, but to be in silence."

The word: *"silence"* denotes quietness.
"To teach" means that Paul does not permit a woman to assume the office of a public teacher in the assembly (Titus 2:3-4 would be an example of private teaching, while 2 Timothy 1:5 would be an example of teaching within the family).

We are equally important within the assembly, but God made us for different roles and responsibilities. In the church as well as in the home, God has given the leadership to men. Indeed, in Chapter 3, we have:

(3) DUTY DEFINED
Chapter 3

Everything rises or falls with leadership, whether it be a family or a local church. If the local church is to do its task effectively, it must have leadership and this implies organization. Do you know what constitutes a New Testament church? Well, according to Philippians 1 verse 1, it is comprised of saints, ruled by godly elders and served by faithful deacons. You see, Paul is speaking here of the church and its duties:

(a) In Relation to Elders
Chapter 3 verses 1-7

Different terms are used in the New Testament for church leaders: *"pastor"*, *"elder"* and *"bishop"*. They all refer to the same office (Acts 20:17, 28 and Titus 1:5, 7).

"Elder" is a translation of the Greek word: *"presbyteros"*. It is translated *"presbytery"* in 1 Timothy 4 verse 14. It simply means an older mature person.

"Bishop" comes from the Greek word: *"episkopos"* and means *"overseer"*.

The local pastor then was an *elder* in terms of spiritual *maturity* and an *overseer* in terms of *ministry*. It was usual for churches to have more than one elder or pastor. The qualifications given here by the Lord are very high, but they do not include what seems so important in so many churches today - success in business or having climbed the social ladder. A milkman or a doctor can serve in the church as long as he has been gifted by God!

His Personal Qualifications

"Blameless" does not mean sinless. It means: *"that cannot be laid hold of"*. That is, there is nothing the enemy can lay hold of to hinder the work or ruin the witness.

"The husband of one wife" means: *"a one woman man"*, morally pure.

"Vigilant" means: *"temperate"*.

"Sober" means: *"self-control"*.

"Of good behaviour" means: *"orderly"*.

"Given to hospitality" means: *"to love strangers"*.

"Apt to teach" - that is, one who works hard in his studies and proclamation (1 Timothy 5:17). This is the one qualification that sets him apart from the deacons.

"Not given to wine" means he does not have a reputation as a drinker.

"No striker" – the man does not use physical force.

"Not greedy of filthy lucre" means he must not be money hungry.

"Patient" means: *"long-suffering"*.

"Not a brawler" means: *"not contentious"*.

"Not covetous" means: *"free from covetousness"*. He has Christ first in his life.

His Family Qualifications

In verse 4 it is clear that the elder should be the head of his household, ruling his own house well.

His Church Qualifications

He must not be a new convert. If he is, Satan may puff him up with pride. The elders must have a good testimony even among the unsaved lest his bad reputation tear down the witness of the church.

It is not easy to serve as a pastor or elder but it is much easier if your character is all God wants it to be.

Then Paul speaks of the church and its duties:

(b) In Relation to Deacons
Chapter 3 verses 8-13

The section begins: *"Likewise"*. This indicates that God has equally important standards for the deacon. The English word: *"deacon"* simply means: *"servant"*. But please notice that the qualifications for this noble office are in many respects similar to those of an elder. Paul talks about:

His Character

He must be *"grave"* (*"dignified"*), *"not doubletongued"* (not a tale-bearer, speaking one thing to one person and something different to another).
"Not given to much wine, not greedy of filthy lucre."

His Convictions

He must be sound in his doctrinal beliefs and sincere and conscientious in his Christian witness.

His Calling

A deacon must first be proved before being appointed to this exalted office. He must be of sterling character and his life both in the home and the world must be beyond reproach.

Do you notice that word *"use"* in verse 10?

"And let these also first be proved; then let them use the office of a deacon."

This tells us that the deacon's office is to be used not just filled.

If you are just going to fill a post rather than exercise a ministry, you would be better not in it at all.

His Companion

His wife also must be dignified, discreet and thoroughly trustworthy.

His Conduct

His moral and parental standards must be above reproach and are identical with those of an elder.

Is it not a serious matter to serve the Lord in the local church? Do we not need to search our own hearts to ensure that we are qualified and fit for such service?

(c) In relation to Members
Chapter 3 verses 14-16

In this closing section of Chapter 3, Paul shows the importance of the local church by describing it under three pictures.

It is: *"the house of God"*.
That speaks of *our Family* and Paul wrote this letter to teach us how to behave as members of God's family.

It is: *"the pillar and ground of truth"*.
That speaks of *our Function*. We are to uphold the truth in an age of apostasy.

It is: *"the body of Christ"*.
That speaks of *our Focus*. This closing verse is perhaps an early Christian hymn, memorized by the saints for their worship services. It is a summary of the person and work of the Lord Jesus and the idea is that the local church should bear witness to Him.

Is this not an exciting challenge? For your local church to witness of Christ to lost sinners at home and abroad? This, says Paul, is our calling.

(4) DANGER DECLARED
Chapter 4

Paul had warned the Ephesian elders that false teachers would invade the church (Acts 20:28-31) and now they had arrived. Here we have:

(a) The Description of False Teachers
Chapter 4 verses 1-5

"Some shall depart from the faith" (verse 1).

They are marked by apostasy. That is what the word: *"depart"* means. It is a wilful turning away from the truth of the Christian faith.

An apostate is not someone struggling to believe but one who wilfully abandons the biblical faith he had once professed.

Paul also points out the source of this apostasy. The source is not *"the growing intelligence of scholars"*, but the satanic influence of demons so that professed believers deny the basic doctrines of the Bible.

Do you notice that they were teaching a false piety? Namely, *abstaining from marriage and abstaining from meat.* They taught that an unmarried life was more spiritual than a married life – and the Roman Catholic Church has been guilty of this. They forbid their priests to marry. These teachers also taught that certain meats were taboo, that if you eat them you are not spiritual. The fact that God called His own creation: *"good"* did not interest these teachers! (Genesis 1:10,12, 18, 21, 25)

Beware of any teaching that tampers with God's institution of marriage and beware of any teaching that tampers with God's creation. God in His Word has declared that all foods are clean (Genesis 1:29-31; Genesis 9:3; Mark 7:14-23 and 1 Corinthians 10:23-26) and through prayer the Christian thanks God and eats the food to His glory (1 Corinthians 10:31).

In contrast to these false teachers, Paul gives us:

(b) The Description of Faithful Teachers
Chapter 4 verses 6-16

A godly under-shepherd will:

- warn church members concerning apostasy (verse 6)
- keep spiritually fit (verses 7-11)
- be a godly role model in all that he does (verse 12)
- continue to publicly read, teach and preach the Word of God (verse 13)
- give himself wholly to the ministry (verse 15)
- keep close check on his own life (verse 16)

As you review this passage, you can see that Paul expected Timothy to build the church. On what? The Word of God. To study it, to teach it and to live it.

Timothy was to be like the blessed man of Psalm 1: *"his delight is in the law of the LORD; and in His law doth he meditate day and night"* (verse 2).

A Journey Through The Bible

Wise are the churches that seek to protect their pastors' time so that they have opportunity to study and pray.
Happy are the men who spend time in the Word. They will not only grow themselves. They will help the churches to grow.

Finally:

(5) DIRECTION DISCLOSED
Chapter 5 - Chapter 6

In these closing chapters Paul gives direction:

(a) IN RELATION TO THE PEOPLE OF GOD

Did you know that the first problem in the early church was a modern one? A group of church members felt neglected by the pastoral team (Acts 6:1). As a result, men were selected to look after the practical affairs so that the apostles could attend to prayer and the ministry of the Word.

Here Paul gives Timothy some instruction in relation to older saints (1 Timothy 5:1-2); to widows (1 Timothy 5:3-16); to elders (1 Timothy 5:17-25); to slaves (1 Timothy 6:1-2) and to the rich (1 Timothy 6:17-19).

But then he gives direction:

(b) IN RELATION TO THE MAN OF GOD

Do you see what Paul calls this young pastor? *"But thou, O man of God"* (1 Timothy 6:11)

What an encouragement to this young, timid, reticent servant of God.

But do you see the three exhortations? *Flee, follow and fight.*

Flee - Sometimes the best thing that a Christian can do is run. Is this not what Joseph did when Potiphar's wife tempted him in Genesis 39?

Is this not one of the things that often brings pastors down? *There are girls, then there is gold* (1 Timothy 6:10) *and there is glory. But we have got to flee.*

Then we must *follow* and then we must *fight*. Paul points to the wonderful example of Christ when He made His courageous witness before Pilate.

"We serve the King of Kings", says Paul. *"Be faithful Timothy until He comes and when He comes He will honour you for your good work."*

What a message Timothy has for our day. We too are called to guard the gospel.

Some people want to ritualize the gospel, some people want to socialize the gospel, some people want to rationalize the gospel and some people want to politicize the gospel.

But we are called upon to guard the gospel.

Paul says elsewhere: *"I am set for the defence of the gospel"* (Philippians 1:17). That gospel God gave to Paul, who in turn committed it to Timothy, who in turn was to guard it and pass it on to others.

Is this not the task of the church? Is this not your task and mine?

Forget about popularity. Keep your eyes on the Judgment Seat of Christ.

Charles Wesley put it like this:

> *A charge to keep I have,*
> *A God to glorify,*
> *A never-dying soul to save,*
> *And fit it for the sky.*

To serve the present age,
My calling to fulfil:
Oh, may it all my pow'rs engage
To do my Master's will!

Arm me with jealous care,
As in Thy sight to live;
And now Thy servant, Lord, prepare
A strict account to give!

Help me to watch and pray,
And on Thyself rely,
Oh, let me not my trust betray,
But press to realms on high.

CHAPTER 16

2 Timothy

If you knew you were about to die, what do you think you would say? The last words of dying people have always fascinated me. They are so revealing of a person's mind, heart and soul.

P.T. Barnum, the famous circus showman, said: *"How were the receipts today at Madison Square Garden?"*

The dying infidel Voltaire cried out: *"I must die abandoned of God and of men".*

D.L. Moody, the American evangelist, said: *"Earth is receding, Heaven is opening, God is calling and I must go".*

Some of the last words of the Cornish evangelist, Billy Bray, were: *"Glory, glory, I'm going to Heaven. Incidentally, Doctor, will you meet me there?"*

The great Baptist preacher, Charles Spurgeon, said as his last words: *"Jesus died for me".*

John Wesley, the founder of Methodism, said: *"Best of all, God is with us".*

As Dr Martyn Lloyd-Jones was dying in 1981, he said: *"Do not keep me back from Glory!"*

The great Bohemian reformer, John Huss, was burned at the stake as a heretic, in Constance, Germany. He said: *"You may cook the goose today ('Huss' in Bohemian means: "goose") but God shall raise up a gander and him you'll never roast."* Did you know that the name *"Luther"* is derived in German from the word: *"gander"*? Martin Luther had not even been born at the time!

However, some of the greatest words ever uttered by a man about to die came from the lips of the apostle Paul. The year was about A.D. 68 and Paul was in what is known as the Mamertine Prison in Rome. This man who once travelled the world telling thousands of people how to know the Lord is now confined in a dingy space about twenty feet in diameter. This place was known as *"the sepulchre"* for many in it were being slowly eaten alive by rats.

So, here is Paul in this small space which is filled with sewage and vermin. He knows that he will soon be with the Lord and he wants to pass the torch of the gospel to this young man Timothy. He says: *"I have fought a good fight, I have finished my course, I have kept the faith"* (2 Timothy 4:7). His race was finished. His warfare was accomplished. But the work of God must go on.

When Moses died, God had to raise up a Joshua.
When Elijah was caught up to heaven, God had to raise up an Elisha.
When Paul died, God had to raise up a Timothy.

Says Dr. Alan Cairns:

"This is the great burden of this epistle. I think of it as the changing of the guard. Paul was dying and Timothy was rising up to stand in his place at least in some measure."

Truly, this great servant of God is at the end of the road. Here, as it were, Paul was *"laying down his arms that Timothy might take them up"*. So these last words of Paul breathe an atmosphere of great solemnity. I find it impossible to read them without being profoundly stirred.

In order for us to understand this book, I want you to notice:

1. THE *WHERE* OF THIS LETTER

As already intimidated, this letter was written from a Roman prison shortly before Paul's death. Paul was released from his first Roman imprisonment for a short period of ministry during which he wrote 1 Timothy and Titus. The book of Titus tells us that Paul visited Nicopolis (Titus 3:12). He must have departed from there and gone to Troas where he abode in the home of Carpus (2 Timothy 4:13). During the period of Paul's release, a great fire destroyed more than half of the city of Rome. *It is said that the Emperor Nero started the fire but that he falsely accused the Christians. Thus began a most terrible persecution of the Christian church.* It is possible that Paul, the leading figure among the believers, was arrested at Troas where in *"a quick exit"* he left his cloak, books and parchments with his host Carpus. He was now a hated prisoner in a Roman prison.

This second imprisonment was far different from his first.

He was then a political prisoner awaiting trial, he is now a condemned criminal awaiting death.
In his first detention he lived in his own hired house, now he is huddled up in a cold, dark, damp dungeon.
During his first imprisonment he was visited by many, now he is forsaken by all.

As we read this final letter from Paul's heart we can sense his loneliness and heartache as he faced trial and certain martyrdom. Nevertheless, Paul was absolutely sure that the Lord was with him, even though many believers had now departed from him.

2. THE *WHY* OF THIS LETTER

As the last letter ever penned by Paul, it is, therefore, a kind of last will and testament.

There are *Personal Wishes* here, as Paul requests Timothy to come to him without delay. He says: *"Come before winter"* (2 Timothy 4:21), come before the time for sailing is past. Do you see how he refers to Timothy? *"My dearly beloved son"* (2 Timothy 1:2). It seems that Timothy was the nearest thing that Paul ever had to a family of his own. There was a relationship with Timothy that was special and it is probable that Paul saw Timothy as his deputy in spite of the difference in temperament and background.

There are *Pastoral Warnings* here. Paul, aware that the end was near, exhorted Timothy to:

- continue faithful in his duties (2 Timothy 1:6)
- hold on to sound doctrine (2 Timothy 1:13-14)
- avoid error (2 Timothy 2:15-18)
- accept persecution for the gospel (2 Timothy 3:10-12)
- put his confidence in Scripture and preach it fearlessly (2 Timothy 3:15 - 4:5).

There are also Parting Words here as Paul says: "Farewell!" to his son in the faith. He encourages him to take up the baton of truth and wield it fearlessly in a godless world.

Indeed, that is:

3. THE *WHAT* OF THIS LETTER

The message of 2 Timothy is: *"guard the gospel"*. Paul sees defeat and apostasy all around him, so he says to Timothy: *"O Timothy, keep that which is committed to thy trust"* (1 Timothy 6:20). The word: *"keep"* means: *"guard"*. *"Guard that which is committed to thy trust."* What was committed to Timothy's trust? What was the deposit? The gospel.

The time of Paul's own departure is now at hand, and as he looks back over the years he can say: *"I have fought a good fight, I have finished my course, I have kept (held intact) the faith"*. But what of the future? Well, now he gives this solemn charge to his dearest son in the faith. With a new sense of responsibility, Timothy is now to guard this priceless vital *"deposit"* of Christian truth.

He is to preserve it, protect it and proclaim it.

Now there are four chapters in this book and Paul, it seems, says to Timothy four things:

(1) FUNCTION WELL
Chapter 1

Fulfil your role, your ministry!

Do you recall what Timothy's name means? *"One who honours God."* We can almost hear Paul saying: *"My dearly beloved son, live up to your name"*. You see, Timothy was indeed a son to Paul. If Paul had been blessed with a son, he would have wanted a son like Timothy. Timothy, whose father seems to have died when he was young, found in Paul the finest father that any young man could ever have.

As Paul's apostolic delegate in Ephesus, Timothy, a young man, functioned as a pastor, a teaching elder, to older people (1 Timothy 4:12 and Chapter 5:1-2) and this was not easy to do. Timothy greatly missed Paul and wanted to quit (1 Timothy 1:3 and 2 Timothy 1:4). Timothy had to deal with false teachers and they are not easily silenced (1 Timothy 1:3).

Moreover, Timothy had physical problems (1 Timothy 5:23) and you get the impression that some of the church members were not giving their pastor the proper respect as God's servant (1 Timothy 4:12 and 2 Timothy 2:6-8). All of these things can have a demoralizing effect so Paul is saying to Timothy: *"Function well!"*

He wants Timothy:

(a) TO DEVELOP HIS FAITH
Chapter 1 verses 3-6

This man who was facing martyrdom took time to pray for Timothy. Paul, who was now facing death, was thinking about: *"the promise of life which is in Christ Jesus"* (verse 1). He reminds Timothy that there was a lot to be thankful for in spite of the problems he was facing.

When Paul came to Lystra on his first missionary journey, Timothy was saved (Acts 14). When he returned on his second missionary journey, Timothy was enlisted for service (Acts 16:3). Paul had watched Timothy's life and service during the years they were together and he was sure that Timothy's faith was genuine. But, while he expresses thanks for Timothy's faith, he seeks to strengthen that faith by reminding him of the faith of his mother and grandmother.

You see, there is not only faith for salvation but there is faith for daily living and Christian service. We need to develop our faith.

Paul also wants Timothy:

(b) TO DISPEL HIS FEARS
Chapter 1 verses 7-12

One of Timothy's problems was cowardice, a timidity about facing problems and doing God's work. He was quite different from Paul! Timothy was neglecting the gift that God had given him (1 Timothy 4:14). He needed to stir it up as a man would fan into flame the embers of a dying fire.

Many Christians are immensely gifted and tremendously blessed, but have fears stifled you and kept you from receiving all that God has in store for you? Like Timothy, are you losing your zeal for the Lord and His work?

Do you recall where Paul was when he wrote this letter? In prison, waiting to be executed. But he says: *"Timothy, don't be ashamed of me or the gospel"* (2 Timothy 1:8).

Are there fears that are affecting you right now?

Is it the fear of ill-health?
The fear of loneliness?
The fear of failure?
The fear of your children turning out wrong?
The fear of not finding the right partner in life?
Zig Ziglar says that fear, F-E-A-R, is often: **"False Evidence which Appears Real"**.

Do you know what you need to do with your fears?

Appropriate the Resources of God! The Holy Spirit (2 Timothy 1:7) does not generate fear in us but rather power, love and discipline. *Acknowledge the Purpose of God!* Suffering is all part of our heavenly calling (2 Timothy 1:8-9). *Appreciate the Son of God!* Christ is faithful and able to keep His own. Do you see verse 12 of 2 Timothy 1?

"For the which cause I also suffer these things: nevertheless I am not ashamed: for I know whom I have believed, and am persuaded that He is able to keep that which I have committed unto Him against that day."

Paul does not say: *"I know what I have believed"*, even though no-one knew better than Paul the glorious truths of the gospel. He says: *"I know whom"*.

Warren Wiersbe says there is a contrast here worth noting. In verse 12, Paul says Christ in glory is able to keep what we give to Him. In verse 14, Paul says the Holy Spirit on earth helps us to keep what Christ gives to us.

Why are you fearful?

> You have the Spirit of God to enable you.
> You have the Purpose of God to enlighten you.
> You have the Son of God to keep you.

So Paul wants Timothy:

(c) TO DISPLAY HIS FAITHFULNESS
Chapter 1 verses 13-18

Doctrinally

"Hold fast the form of sound words, which thou hast heard of me, in faith and love which is in Christ Jesus. That good thing which was committed unto thee keep by the Holy Ghost which dwelleth in us" (2 Timothy 1:13-14).

The word *"form"* in verse 13 means: *"outline"*. The early church had an outline of sound, healthy doctrine. The Lord had given this deposit of spiritual truth to Paul (1 Timothy 1:11) and he had given it to Timothy (1 Timothy 6:20). It was now Timothy's solemn responsibility to *"hold fast"*, *"to guard"* the precious deposit of Christian truth and pass it on to others (2 Timothy 2:2).

Do you see what Paul is saying?

"Timothy, I am dying. My generation of preachers is over. Now it is time for you to step forward. It is time for you to be on the front line, to take up the torch of truth for the cause of Christ."

What a challenge this is for us **locally**! Time will bring changes in our local churches shortly. The old guard is passing, but where are the young men who know the book, live the book, preach the book and who will not compromise on the Word of God? Where are the young men who will not just be office-bearers in name but in nature?

What a challenge this is for us **nationally**! One generation of preachers passes. Men who blazed a trail for God are now passing away. Hence the need for faithful pastors is great.

Practically

Dr. Sidlow Baxter points out that the *"some"* of 1 Timothy has become the *"all"* in 2 Timothy. In his first letter, for example, Paul says: *"Some have turned aside"* (1 Timothy 1:6) and *"Some have made shipwreck"* (1 Timothy 1:19). But look at 2 Timothy 1 verse 15: *"All they which are in Asia be turned away from me"*. Do you see the *"all"*? In 2 Timothy 4 verse 16, Paul says: *"All men forsook me"*. You would have thought that the Asian believers would have stood by Paul but instead they forsook him.

One man, however, came to Rome. He sought Paul and served him without fear or shame. His name was Onesiphorus, and he is mentioned in verse 16. "Onesiphorus" means: *"profit-bearing"* - and what a profitable friend he was to Paul. What did he do? *"He oft refreshed me."*

Do you know any believer like that?

I know Christians and I could say of them: *"He often rebuked me, reproached me, rejected me!"* Do you *"refresh"* others? The Greek word means: *"to cool again".* The Amplified Bible says: *"Bracing me like fresh air".*

Do you know Christians like that?

In midst of their trials, they minister to you and they are like a breath of fresh air.

(2) FOCUS WELL
Chapter 2

A man attended a convention, wearing two badges. When asked why, he said: *"Oh, I'm having an identity crisis!"*

Paul did not want Timothy to have an identity crisis, so he explained what a pastor, elder, teacher, believer is and does.

Timothy was:

(a) TO BE A STEWARD
Chapter 2 verses 1-2

"Thou therefore, my son, be strong in the grace that is in Christ Jesus. And the things that thou hast heard of me among many witnesses, the same commit thou to faithful men, who shall be able to teach others also."

The word *"commit"* means: *"deposit"* and, of course, refers to the treasure of gospel truth that God had committed to Paul (1 Timothy 1:11); that Paul had committed to Timothy (1 Timothy 6:20) and that Timothy was to commit to others.

Do you see here the four stages in the handing on of the truth that Paul envisages? From Christ to Paul, from Paul to Timothy, from Timothy to faithful men, from faithful men to others also.

Is this not the responsibility of elders? Handing on the torch of truth? Training faithful men to reach others.

There are two things that every pastor/elder must face at the end of his ministry. Did I keep the faith? Did I pass that gospel on to others in its undiluted purity?

(b) TO BE A SOLDIER
Chapter 2 verses 3-4

"Thou therefore endure hardness, as a good soldier of Jesus Christ. No man that warreth entangleth himself with the affairs of this life; that he may please Him who hath chosen him to be a soldier."

Do you recall Timothy's call to service?

"Him would Paul have to go forth with him" (Acts 16:3). The words: *"go forth"* literally mean: *"to take to the field as a soldier".* This was Timothy's enlistment. Of course, every Christian is a soldier in God's army - it is just that some troops are loyal and some are not. Was Timothy discouraged because of the opposition he was facing? Did he forget that the Christian life is not a playground but a battleground?

We are in a battle and we must be willing to concentrate as well as to suffer. Where would every army be if every soldier had part-time work that took him away from his military duties? Pastors, elders and missionaries who spend more time on their business ventures than on the work of the Lord are dividing their interests and weakening their ministries.

(c) TO BE A SUCCESS
Chapter 2 verses 5-7

"And if a man also strive for masteries, yet is he not crowned, except he strive lawfully. The husbandman that laboureth must be first partaker of the fruits. Consider what I say; and the Lord give thee understanding in all things."

Timothy was to develop *the persistence of the athlete* (verse 5) and *the patience of the farmer* (verses 6-7).

The phrase: *"to strive lawfully"* comes from a Greek phrase: *"athlein nomimos"* used to describe the professional athlete, the man whose struggle was no part-time affair. From a human standpoint, Paul was a loser. There was no-one in the grandstands cheering him, yet Paul was a winner for he had kept the rules laid down in the Word of God. One day, he would get his reward from Jesus Christ.

As for the farmer, of all occupations his calls for patience. There are no quick results! Timothy was not to be discouraged if the harvest failed to come immediately. Do you recall James' words? *"Be patient therefore, brethren, unto the coming of the Lord. Behold, the husbandman waiteth for the precious fruit of the earth, and hath long patience for it, until he receive the early and latter rain"* (James 5:7).

One pastor wisely said: *"The harvest is not the end of the meeting - it is the end of the age"*.

So do you see what Timothy is to be? A steward, a soldier, a success – and:

(d) TO BE A SUFFERER
Chapter 2 verses 8-13

Paul talks here about the experience of Christ (verse 8), then of himself as an apostle (verses 9-10) and then of Christian believers (verses 11-13). What an encouragement the Lord Jesus is to a suffering Christian soldier! He died and rose again - proving that suffering leads to glory and that seeming defeat leads to victory.

Many believers around the world suffer persecution and danger. More Christians were tortured and put to death for Christ's sake in the 20th Century than in any other time in history. The 21st Century is shaping up to be even worse. The suffering you face may not be physical, but is it mental, emotional or spiritual? Is your faith being ridiculed? Are you being excluded because of your moral stand? Then don't forget Christ's victorious conquest (verse 8); God's unfettered Word (verse 9) and God's dependable promises (verses 11-13).

Many scholars say verses 11 to 13 may have been an early Christian hymn or confession of faith.

"It is a faithful saying: For if we be dead with Him, we shall also live with Him: If we suffer, we shall also reign with Him: if we deny Him, He also will deny us: If we believe not, yet He abideth faithful: He cannot deny Himself."

It stresses the Christian's oneness with Christ: when He died, we died with Him as members of His body, we arose with Him and we shall reign with Him.

You see, our unbelief will not cancel the faithfulness of God.

An unsaved person asked an old Christian: *"Are you not afraid that you will slip through His fingers?"*
"How can I?" she replied.
"I am one of His fingers."
She understood that she was part of the body of Christ.

Timothy was also:

(e) TO BE A STUDENT
Chapter 2 verses 14-19

As a student, he is to study the Word of God (verse 15) and as a student, he is to shun the words of men (verses 16-19). The pastor, teacher or elder is to be a workman in God's Word. Now, how is he to handle *"the word of truth"*? *Diligently!* That is what the word *"study"* means. Many pastors are so involved in administration, committees, and so on that they have little time left for study. Yet the ministry demands total commitment, everything that a man has to give.

Dr. Graham Scroggie said to the elders of a church where he had just commenced his ministry: *"What do you want? My feet or my head? For you cannot have both".*

How are we to handle the Word of Truth? *Carefully! "Rightly dividing!*" It implies cutting through the Word carefully, the way an engineer builds a road.

How are we to handle the Word of Truth? *Accurately!* Not like bad workmen like Hymenaeus and Philetus who taught that the resurrection had already taken place. Every local church should be a Bible school where the Word of God is taught accurately.

Finally, Timothy was:

(f) TO BE A SERVANT
Chapter 2 verses 20-26

Paul describes the local church as a house with a solid foundation and containing vessels of different kinds. Some are vessels of high honour, others have much more mundane uses, but all are important.

Paul was a *"chosen vessel"* (Acts 9:15). Timothy could never be a Paul, but in his own sphere with his own gift, he was to be just as much a vessel *"meet for the master's use"* (2 Timothy 2:21).

We do not all have the same capacity or gifts, but we can all be useful to the Saviour. The important thing is that we are clean vessels. Do you want to serve the Lord acceptably? Are you clean? Are you dedicated unto God? Are you marked by purity, gentleness, patience and meekness?

Are you focussed on what God has called you to be?

(3) FIGHT WELL
Chapter 3

The chapter commences:

"This know also, that in the last days perilous times shall come."

Generally that phrase: *"the last days"* means the period that began with the ministry of Christ on earth (Hebrews 1:1-2), but specifically: *"the last days"* seem to refer to the state of the church before the coming of Christ. The word *"perilous"* means: *"difficult, hard to deal with"*. This is the same word used in Matthew 8 verse 28 to describe the two demoniacs who met Christ when He visited the country of the Gergesenes. The demoniacs are described as: *"exceeding fierce"*. Paul is pointing to that time when wickedness will come to full flower and fruit and we can see the beginning of that age today.

Do you see what Paul saw here?

(a) THE PERIL OF APOSTASY
Chapter 3 verses 1-9

Paul's description of self-loving (verse 2) rather than God-loving humanity is tragically illustrated in the columns of our daily newspapers.
"Having a form of godliness" suggests an outward appearance of religion not true Christian faith. They have never experienced the power of God in their lives. This is *form without force*. This is *religion without reality*.
Paul issues a warning: *"From such turn away"* (verse 5).

Do we put a distance between ourselves and superficial professors of Christianity?

How are to deal with opposition to the truth from without and a departure from the faith within? Well, do you see here:

(b) THE PROTECTION FROM APOSTASY
Chapter 3 verses 10-17

Paul urges Timothy to be patient in suffering (verses 10-14) and persistent in truth (verses 15-17).

"Timothy, remember the way I behaved. You've seen how I endured all the trials that came my way. Remember that if you're patient in suffering and you continue holding to the truth of God's Word, you'll find your way safely through all the perils and pitfalls of this collapsing world."

What do we need in an age of apostasy? We need a return to the Word of God. *The only answer to Satan's lies is God's truth.* If every local church would go back to the Word of God, and every teacher would teach the Word of God, Satan's disciples would be defeated. The answer for our age, for our day, for our generation, for our country is the Word of God.

What a testimony to the origin of the Bible is given in verses 16 and 17.

"All Scripture is given by inspiration of God."

Beware of the man who stands in the pulpit and says: *"The Bible contains the Word of God"*. No, it does not! *The Bible IS the Word of God.*

The Greek term for *"inspiration"* here is *"theopneustos"*. It means: *"God breathed"*. Literally, the verse says: *"All Scripture is God breathed"*.

It means that the words of the Bible are the words of God Himself. Every Scripture was breathed out by God. You see, *when the Scripture speaks, God speaks. When God speaks, the Scripture speaks.* Do you want to know how you fight apostasy? Let the Scripture loose.

Charles Spurgeon said:

"Truth is like a lion. Whoever thought of defending a lion? Turn it loose and it will defend itself."

(4) FINISH WELL
Chapter 4

Didn't Paul finish well? Here is the great apostle writing these words to his son in the faith. He is writing within weeks, perhaps days, of his martyrdom. According to a fairly reliable tradition, Paul was beheaded on the Ostian Way in Rome. He is saying: *"I am dying. My day is over. Follow my example"*. You see, Paul wants Timothy to finish well:

(a) DOCTRINALLY
Chapter 4 verses 1-5

Paul says in verse 2: *"Preach the Word"*. Not merely preach around the Word and about the Word. Expound the Word. Get to the heart of the Word of God.

Preach it Clearly: the word *"preach"* here means: *"to preach like a herald"*. The herald was commissioned by the ruler to make his announcements in a loud clear voice so everyone could hear.

Charles Spurgeon said to his students: *"God gives to a preacher a voice!"*

Preach it Urgently: *"be instant"* means: to be urgent, especially in giving the gospel to sinners. They are on their way to hell!

Preach it Relevantly: *"reprove, rebuke, exhort with all longsuffering and doctrine"*.

Why must we preach the Word? Look at verses 3 and 4:

"For the time will come when they will not endure sound doctrine; but after their own lusts shall they heap to themselves teachers, having itching ears; And they shall turn away their ears from the truth, and shall be turned unto fables."

That time is already here! Many church attenders do not want *"healthy"* sound doctrine. They want religious entertainment. They want a string of little stories to make folk laugh or cry at the right time. But Paul says: *"Preach the Word"*.

Does this generation not need a new race of godly preachers?

To quote Alan Cairns again:

"The old guard is passing, our need is for new men of the old school, men of the apostolic mould who will 'guard the deposit.'"

(b) EMOTIONALLY
Chapter 4 verses 6-9

"I am now ready to be offered, and the time of my departure is at hand" (verse 6).

Paul knows that his days are numbered by the hours and his hours by the minutes. *But he is not ashamed and he is not afraid.* There is no fear of the shadow of death, just faith in the Shepherd of life. The word: *"departure"* means: *"a loosing from"* or: *"a release"*.

This is what death is for the Christian.

It's a release; it's a laying down of the burden to rest; it's striking camp in order to go home; it's a setting sail for glory; it's the answer to all life's queries.

It would appear that for the believer the very best thing that can happen to him is to die (Philippians 1:23).

Do you fear death? Well, think of it as a departure, a setting sail for glory, a release from the burdens of life, a going home to the Father's house, faith turning to sight, when you see His face.

(c) PERSONALLY
Chapter 4 verses 10-16

Why was this? Look at verse 10:

"Demas hath forsaken me, having loved this present world, and is departed unto Thessalonica; Crescens to Galatia, Titus unto Dalmatia."

Some in Paul's circle were not faithful and he could not depend on them. Demas had forsaken him. Alexander had persecuted him. Maybe it was Alexander who betrayed him and told the Roman authorities that he was in Troas. The believers in Rome and at Ephesus who could have stood with him had failed him in his hour of need (verse 16). But Paul knew that Timothy would not fail him. So he says to Timothy: *"Come before winter"*, before the shipping season would end. If he delayed, Paul would be dead.

If you want to finish well personally, do not be disappointed at the failure of others and thank God for the encouragement of others.

(d) SPIRITUALLY
Chapter 4 verses 17-22

How do you finish well spiritually?

In verse 16, Paul says:

"At my first answer no man stood with me, but all men forsook me."

Was Paul the only Christian as he stood in Nero's courtroom? Picture him, the greatest Christian, the greatest scholar, the greatest missionary, the greatest theologian in history and as he looks round, he says:

"At my first answer no man stood with me."

So, how do you finish well spiritually?

Rest in the Presence of God

"Notwithstanding the Lord stood with me" (verse 17).

Continue with the Work of God

Paul wanted to preach the Word so that the Gentiles might be saved (verse 17).

Live to the Glory of God

Paul's greatest fear was not death. It was that he might do something that would dishonour God's name (verse 18).

Vance Havner said:

"I'd like to get home before dark."

Although you're saved, you're never safe as far as your testimony is concerned until you get home.

Paul finished well.

Was Timothy able to visit him before he died? We are not sure but tradition has it that Timothy was in Ephesus for many years as one of the pastors, one of the teaching elders, of the church.

Late in the first century, during the reign of Emperor Nerva (A.D. 96-98), a public demonstration for the god Dionysus was held in Ephesus. This event included public sinful activity. Timothy was so torn of heart by the events that he stood up and started shouting in opposition to this public frenzy. When he did that, the mob became enraged, picked up clubs and stones, and beat Timothy until he died. He finished well.

In 1904, William Borden, a member of the Borden dairy family, finished high school in Chicago and was given a world cruise as a graduation present. While travelling through the Near East and the Far East, he became greatly burdened for the lost. After returning home, he spent seven years at Princeton University, the first four in undergraduate work and the last three in seminary.

While in school, he penned these words in the back of his Bible: **"No reserves!"**

Although his family pleaded with him to take control of the business, which was struggling, he insisted that God's call to the mission field had priority.

After disposing of his wealth, he added: **"No retreat!"** after the words: **"No reserves!"**

On his way to China to witness to Muslims there, he contracted cerebral meningitis in Egypt and died within a month.

After his death, someone looking through his Bible discovered these final words: **"No regrets!"**

He knew that the Lord does not require success, only faithfulness.

Finishing Well.

How will you finish? **"No reserves, no retreat, no regrets"** ?

May the Lord give us the grace to finish well.

CHAPTER 17

Titus

Someone has said that many people are like wheel barrows. No good unless pushed!

Some are like canoes. They have to be paddled!

Some are like kites. If you do not keep them on a string, they fly away!

Some are like footballs. You cannot tell which way they will bounce next!

Some are like balloons. Full of wind and ready to blow up!

Some are like trailers. They have to be pulled!

But, some are like a good watch. *Open face, pure gold, quietly busy and full of good works.*

What are you like?

We all should be like a good watch. Titus was – and like him, we should acknowledge God's authority and accept His assignment.

There are 13 references to Titus in the Bible. His name means: *"pleasing"* and, indeed, he was one who brought much pleasure to the heart of Paul. But who was he? Well, let us consider firstly:

1. THE PERSON

Paul, in verse 4 of the opening chapter, writes: *"To Titus, mine own son after the common faith"*. It is a remarkable fact that Titus is not mentioned in the book of Acts. All we know of Titus we gather from the writings of Paul. Apparently Titus had been won to Christ at an early period in Paul's ministry. We know this because he accompanied Paul and Barnabas as part of the Antioch delegation to settle the matter of Gentile freedom from the ceremonial law (Galatians 2:1-4). We know from the same chapter that Titus was a Gentile, a Greek (Galatians 2:3) and that his home was probably in Antioch (Galatians 2:1).

It is evident that he became a very loyal, valuable assistant to Paul in his ministry. It was Titus whom Paul sent to Corinth to straighten out certain disorders in the church and to initiate an offering for the poor saints at Jerusalem (2 Corinthians 2:12-13 and Chapter 7:6, 13-15). The fact that Paul would entrust him with such a task reveals his spiritual maturity and stability.

Titus later caught up with Paul in Macedonia with good news of the Corinthians (2 Corinthians 7:5-6) and he was sent back bearing 2 Corinthians. He was also charged by Paul to complete the collection for the believers at Jerusalem (2 Corinthians 8:16-17).

After this, little is known of Titus until we read of him in the Pastoral letters.

It seems that after Paul's first Roman imprisonment, Titus accompanied Paul to the island of Crete and there Paul left him to correct the things that were wrong.

Later Titus received this letter from Paul to guide him and support him in his task.

You know, Paul was very wise in the use he made of the young men around him. Think of Timothy and Titus. Both were young, both were gifted and both were appreciated by Paul. Both were sent on delicate and difficult missions - Timothy to Ephesus and Titus to Crete. They were appointed by Paul as *"spiritual trouble-shooters"* to carry out tasks for which he considered them to be suitable.

These two young men were, however, completely different from one another.

Although his father was a Greek, Timothy had been brought up a

Jew, Titus was a pure Gentile. Timothy was circumcised but Titus was not (Galatians 2:3).

Timothy seems to have been younger than Titus.

Titus seems to have been a stronger man, physically and spiritually, than Timothy for Paul seems less concerned about the conduct of Titus and the way others might treat him than he was about Timothy.

Do you know something? How important it is in the Lord's work to have the right man for the job. Here was Titus and he realized that service is always the outcome of salvation.

He would sing:

> *"I will not work my soul to save,*
> *For that my Lord has done,*
> *But I will work like any slave,*
> *For love of God's dear Son."*

2. THE PLACE

In verse 5, Paul refers to Crete.

It is one of the largest islands in the Mediterranean Sea, lying south east of Greece and measuring 160 miles long by 35 miles at its widest. It is mentioned in Acts 27 verse 7 in the account given of the voyage undertaken by Paul on his way to Rome.

Crete was a very difficult place in which to establish a church. The Cretians had a bad reputation. It is described in Titus 1 verses 12-13. Paul quotes a sixth century B.C. Cretian poet by the name of Epimenides who refers to his own people as: *"liars, evil beasts and lazy gluttons"*. Just as calling someone *"Corinthian"* was to describe them as being: *"destitute of morals"* so: *"to cretanize"* meant: *"habitual lying and cheating"*. Not a very promising place for the gospel! Did the gospel reach Crete by those who were present at Jerusalem on the day of Pentecost? (Acts 2:11). Or, was it through Paul and Titus that these island people heard the gospel for the very first time? One thing is sure. Paul had a firm conviction in his heart. He believed that the grace of God that could save him could do the same for anybody anywhere. He was not disappointed for when he and Titus preached the gospel in Crete, they saw people saved and a church was formed. On leaving the island, Paul wrote to encourage and instruct Titus and to *"set in order the things that are wanting"* (Titus 1:5).

Indeed, this was:

3. THE PURPOSE

"For this cause left I thee in Crete, that thou shouldest set in order the things that are wanting, and ordain elders in every city, as I had appointed thee."

These churches were not fully established according to New Testament church principles. Elders were not yet appointed. This was one of the reasons why Paul wrote this letter, but there was more than that.

There was to be godly leadership, but there was also to be godly living.

Paul puts it like this in Chapter 3 and verse 8: *"be careful to maintain good works"*. The subject of *"good works"* is a major emphasis in this book: Chapter 1 verse 16, Chapter 2 verses 7 and 14, Chapter 3 verses 1, 8 and 14.

Saved by grace means saved unto good works.

In 1 Timothy we are to protect the gospel; in 2 Timothy we are to proclaim the gospel, but in Titus we are to practise the gospel.

There ought to be a life of godliness not worldliness (Titus 1:1 and Chapter 2:12). So Paul is writing this letter to establish *godly Leadership,* and *godly Living.*

But I think there is something else here: he is writing to establish *godly Labouring.*

One scholar says:

"God and Christ are regularly referred to as Saviour (Titus 1:3-4; Chapter 2:10 and 13, and Chapter 3:4-6) and the saving plan is so emphasized in Chapter 2 verses 11 to 14 that it indicates the major thrust of the epistle is that of equipping the churches of Crete for effective evangelism."

How do you evangelize effectively? How do you win people who are: *"liars, evil beasts and lazy gluttons"*?

You live before them: *"soberly, righteously, and godly, in this present world"* (Titus 2:12).

Do you know why our evangelism has lost its edge?

> *Our living contradicts our speaking.*
> *Our works do not match our words.*
> *Our conduct is not in keeping with our creed.*
> *Our lifestyle is not in step with our language.*

Remember, we are living epistles, *"known and read of all men"* (2 Corinthians 3:2).

Would you have fancied a position in Crete? It would have been easy for Titus, like many others, to have *"heard God's call to go elsewhere"*, but he stuck it out and finished his work.

Tradition tells that after Paul's death, Titus, who had been with Paul in Rome during his second imprisonment, returned to Crete to continue the work of God until his death at the age of 94.

Now the book of Titus has three chapters and I want to divide our study accordingly:

1. The Organization of the Church
Chapter 1

Some tell us that the church should have no organization for the church is an organism, that is, it is a living body (Colossians

1:18). Well, it *is* an organism. It *is* a living body. Yet, in these Pastoral Epistles we find Paul instructing Timothy and Titus to establish the church into a regular and orderly community. There is meant to be, in the words of Dr. Sidlow Baxter: *"adequate even though simple organization"*. It would seem from this letter that there were a number of churches on the island of Crete. The striking thing seems to be that they were autonomous, that is self-governing.

To again quote Sidlow Baxter:

"It is a significant thing that although the New Testament gives counsels and directions as to the organizing of local assemblies or churches, it nowhere even hints at any central board of administration such as those which have since developed and which exist with such widespread powers today. There may well be voluntary unions of churches which do not infringe local autonomy, but there must be no governing executives, for these while seeming to accomplish a useful outward unity, almost invariably violate and often destroy that inward unity, which comes of free and direct loyalty to the apostolic word."

I agree whole-heartedly with this statement. There was no outside body telling these churches what they should do.

Here is Paul writing to Titus to bring some organization to these local autonomous churches on the island of Crete. What does such organization involve? Well, first and foremost:

(a) GOD's WORD Must be Expounded
Chapter 1 verses 1-4

It is interesting how Paul presents himself in his introduction to this letter.

In relation to the *Father*, he was a *bond slave*; in relation to the *Son*, he was an *apostle* (verse 1); in relation to *Titus*, he was a *spiritual parent* (verse 4), but in relation to the *Word*, he was *preacher* (verse 3).

Do you see the place Paul gives to the Word of God in the life of the local church? Paul talks here about:

The Power of the Word

"Paul, a servant of God, and an apostle of Jesus Christ, according to the faith of God's elect" (verse 1).

The *"faith"* is that body of truth contained in the Word. This *"faith"* is what Jude calls: *"the faith which was once delivered unto the saints"* (Jude 3). It is that deposit of truth that God gave to Paul and which he in turn gave to Timothy and Titus. You see, even our personal salvation commences with an honest reception of the factual and theological statements of the gospel.

How can you be a Christian and deny the deity of Jesus Christ?
How can you be a Christian and deny the sinless perfection of Jesus Christ?
How can you be a Christian and deny the once and for all sacrifice of the Cross?

You cannot!

Paul is talking here about the Word in relation to our salvation.

The Purpose of the Word

"The truth which is after godliness" (verse 1).

The truth of the gospel changes a life from ungodliness to holy living. Was this not one of the problems in Crete? They were, in effect, saying: *"God has saved us by grace so we are free to sin"*. If someone so speaks, if someone believes that they can continue in sin, then it needs to be seriously questioned whether they are truly saved!

Paul answers this teaching from the start by defining the faith as: *"the truth which is after godliness"*.

"Godliness" is a favourite word with Paul. He uses it in 1 Timothy 2 verses 2 and 10, Chapter 3 verse 16, Chapter 4 verses 7 and 8, Chapter 6 verses 3, 5, 6 and 11. He uses it in 2 Timothy 3 verse 5 and again in Titus 1 verse 1. By *"godliness"*, Paul simply means practical holiness in every day life.

Paul is talking here about the Word in relation to our sanctification.

The Priority of the Word

Verse 2 speaks about: *"hope of eternal life"*. How does God reveal His message of *"eternal life"*? Through preaching!

"But hath in due times manifested His word through preaching, which is committed unto me according to the commandment of God our Saviour" (verse 3).

God's ordained method for communicating His Word is not through personal dialogue but through pulpit delivery.

Paul is talking here about the Word in relation to our service.

As you consider this opening paragraph, you can see that Paul related everything in his life to the ministry of the Word of God. Did he not want Timothy to grasp this fact? Did he not want Titus to grasp this fact? He wanted these *"preacher boys"* to make the Word of God a priority in their ministries.

Do *we* not need to get back to the Bible? Do you recall the cry of those in the days of Ezra and Nehemiah? *"Bring the book!"* (Nehemiah 8:1) Is this your desire? Is this the longing of our churches? That the Word might be expounded? That the place of preaching must always be central? That our local churches might be *"Bible schools"* where the Word is taught?

The pulpit is in the centre of our buildings for a very good reason. It is to emphasise the centrality of the Word of God.

(b) GODLY LEADERSHIP Must be Established
Chapter 1 verses 5-9

I wonder if there is a hint here that Titus wanted to resign. There was certainly opposition to his ministry, but if you are going to be a pastor or elder - and be a good one - you need to stand fast and not waver even in difficult times.

A little boy had an old horse, more of a nag than a steed.
A man was making fun of the boy's horse and he asked: *"Son, can he run fast?"*
The boy replied: *"No sir, but he can stand fast".*

Now what we need are some preachers, pastors and elders who can stand fast.

Paul says:

"Titus, this is why I left you in Crete. If there were no problems to solve, the church would not need you."

Titus was there to: "set in order the things that were wanting". "Set in order" is a medical term meaning: *"to set a broken bone or straighten a crooked limb".* That metaphor teaches us that sometimes churches can be broken. Sometimes churches can have problems. One of the elder's requirements is to be a spiritual physician in orthopaedics who can put things together. He is to be a mender of things. He is to show tender loving care for the flock. When things are out of order, he is to put things in order.

Titus was not the spiritual dictator of the island, but he was Paul's official apostolic representative with authority to work. It was Paul's policy to ordain elders in the churches he had established (Acts 14:23). He had not been able to stay long enough in Crete so he says: *"Titus, here is priority number one - ordain elders in every city".*

I am sure you have noticed before the **Plurality that is Stressed.** *"Ordain elders!"* These letters are certainly not a mandate for a one man leadership.

Gender is also Stressed
"The husband of one wife."

Have you also noticed that **Spiritual Character** is emphasised over gift?

Leaders often grumble that their problems would be solved if only the members would follow them. But, is the real problem not really with those of us who are in leadership? Inevitably people subconsciously follow their leaders. They may not follow what the leaders *say*, but they do follow what the leaders *do.*

One of the things that you see as a church leader is this: You see your own strengths and weaknesses appearing in the church.

Is this not why the qualifications of leaders focus more on character than gift?

It is not so much what a leader *can do* that makes him a leader but what *he is* both at home and in public. Is this not why character is more important than ability?

Church leadership is about being a *good model as well as a good manager,* about *being visible as well as being audible.*

Paul uses three words to describe leaders in the church.
'Elders' (verse 5); *'bishop'* (verse 7) and *'steward'* (verse 7).
The word *"elder"* emphasizes *his maturity;* the word *"bishop"* emphasizes his *ministry,* and the word *"steward"* emphasizes his *authority.* In ancient Greek and Roman societies, a *steward* managed a household on behalf of the owner. He had authority.

Notice not only the *names* of an elder, look at the *nature* of an elder. Paul speaks about him:

Morally: *"blameless"* - the word *"blameless"* means: *"unaccused"* and *"irreproachable"*. The idea is that the elder cannot be charged with wrongdoing. There is nothing the enemy can lay hold of to hinder the work or ruin the witness.

Domestically: *"the husband of one wife"* - a one woman man. That makes it impossible for a woman to be an elder!

"Having faithful children not accused of riot or unruly" – some say this may mean the elder's children must be believing children. One thing is sure: if a man's household is not under control, he is an unwise choice to guide the saints (1 Timothy 3:4-5).

Socially: *"blameless"* - above reproach. *"Not self-willed"* - an elder must not be wrapped up in himself, only doing what he does for self-interest. *"Not soon angry"* - he must not be quick-tempered, one with a short fuse and easily provoked. *"Not given to wine"* - he must not be someone who is addicted to wine or strong drink. *"No striker"* – the word literally means: *"fist-fighter"*. *"Not given to filthy lucre"* or: *"Not greedy for gain"* - materialism and covetousness destroy credibility with the flock and distract an elder from his true task of shepherding.

Can you see the elder *morally, domestically* and *socially*? Can you see him:

Spiritually: *"a lover of hospitality"* - hospitality is the gateway to dealing with people's problems as well as offering personal instruction in the faith. *"A lover of good men"* or: *"a lover of what is good"* - and this would include good men. A man is a good man because he has a good heart and because he surrounds himself with good things. *"Sober"* - is prudent. *"Just"* or: *"Upright"* - he is a person of integrity who sticks by his word and practises what he preaches. *"Holy"* - unstained is the idea. *"Temperate"* – means *"self-controlled"*. It applies to a man's appetites and actions.

Can you see the picture that Paul is painting? Can you see the elder *morally, domestically, socially and spiritually*? Look at him now:

Doctrinally: *"Holding fast the faithful word as he hath been taught, that he may be able by sound doctrine both to exhort and to convince the gainsayers"* (verse 9).

The elder must know the Word for two reasons.

He must be able to *Exhort the Saints.* Do you see that word *"exhort"*? It means: *"to call near, to invite"*. Is this not his task? To call people to a closer walk with the Lord?

But he must be able also to *Expose the Rebels.* The word: *"gainsayers"* means: *"those who say against, those who contradict"*. In the context of Titus, it means refuting the false teachers who spread unhealthy doctrine.

We have got to get into the Word. Do you ever hear people say: *"We don't want doctrine. Just give us helpful devotional thoughts"*? Such people do not know what they are saying. Apart from Bible doctrine, there can be no spiritual help or health. I remember a man saying to me: *"I could come on Sunday morning and just look at the text on the wall and go home"*. Did he never read these letters?

The word: *"gainsayers"* can also mean: *"to dispute or to refuse"*. We are never short of those in the church who want to dispute!

I heard about a church member who objected to anything that went on in the church. In every business meeting, he always argued and complained about what was being discussed. One Sunday, the pastor announced that someone had given the church a large and beautiful chandelier. As usual, the man got up and objected to the church taking it.

The pastor said: *"It is being given to us. It is not costing us a single penny. Why would you be against it?"*

The man replied: *"Well, first of all, we don't have anyone who can play it! Secondly, what we need around here is more light!"*

(c) GRAVE ERROR Must Be Exposed
Chapter 1 verses 10-16

What was this error? Well, it was similar to what Timothy had to deal with in Ephesus. Do you see how it is described in verse 14?

"Not giving heed to Jewish fables, and commandments of men, that turn from the truth."

There was in Crete a group of people who contradicted the teachings of Paul and taught instead Jewish fables (legalism) and the commandments of men (traditionalism). Paul describes them further in verse 10 as those *"of the circumcision"*. Were these not the people who had battled with Paul from Jerusalem to Rome? Seeking to add to the gospel. They are still opposing the truth! When we mix law with grace, we end up with false doctrine. The motivation of these false teachers was financial gain (verse 11) and the local people's natural feelings made them easy prey for these charlatans (verse 12).

Dietary laws and asceticism were key doctrines to these false teachers and Paul attacked these people in verse 15:

"Unto the pure all things are pure: but unto them that are defiled and unbelieving is nothing pure; but even their mind and conscience is defiled."

It is sad that this verse has been used by some professing Christians to support their immoral sinful practices. They say: *"'To the pure all things are pure', so what I am doing is not wrong!"* But Paul did not have morals in mind when he wrote these words. These false teachers were teaching that Jewish dietary laws still applied to Christian believers (1 Timothy 4:3-5). They were saying: *"If you ate forbidden food, you defiled yourself, but if you refused that food you became holier"*. Paul says that it is just the opposite! It is not the food which was defiling the teachers. Rather, the teachers were defiling the food. Moral purity is not a matter of diets. It is a matter of a clean heart and a pure conscience (Matthew 6:22-23 and Romans 14:14).

Now how was Titus to treat these false teachers?

He was to:

Reject them (verses 11-12).
Rebuke them (verses 13-14).
Refuse them (verses 15-16).

Are there still not false teachers with us today? Some of them may preach to thousands of people and they will throw in a Bible verse here and here. You could say that they throw in a little Bible, but it is all about positive thinking, how to improve your self-image, how to feel good and how to climb the social ladder. It is pure psychology - and thousands fall for it.

Many say: *"Sure, it makes no difference what you believe just as long as you believe something!"* Well, it makes all the difference between life and death whether or not you believe the truth of the Word or the lies of the Devil (John 8:32).

You can choose what you believe, but you cannot choose the consequences.

2. The Operation of the Church
Chapter 2

If Titus had spent all his time dealing with the false teachers, he would have neglected other matters that are necessary for a healthy church. Warren Wiersbe says: *"Blessed are the balanced!"* It is important that the elders have a balanced ministry, teaching the saints as well as refuting the skeptics. Here Paul deals with different groups in the church and shows us how the church is to act or operate. Notice:

(a) THE PRACTICAL EXHORTATIONS
Verses 1-9

To the Older Saints: (verses 2-3)

Is it not a blessing when a local church has older believers who have long walked with the Lord? These older Christians are privileged to have lived so long but with that privilege comes serious responsibility.

The aged men are to be *sober* or vigilant, *grave,* easy to respect, *temperate,* self-controlled, and *sound* or healthy in the faith. Which do you think is the most important? Physical or spiritual health? Are we who are older *patient* with the younger generation?

The aged women. What an opportunity they have to teach the younger women both by precept and example.

To the Younger Saints (verses 4-8):

The Young Women. She needs to be sober and take a serious attitude to marriage and to the home.

The Young Men. They need to be clean, sincere and serious.

There are also practical exhortations here:

To the Servants (verses 9-10):

Paul warned these Christian slaves about three sins they must avoid. Disobedience, talking back and stealing. There are no slaves today, but what about us as employees? Do we obey orders? Do we talk back? Do we steal from our employers?

Paul gave a good reason why a Christian employee should be trustworthy: *"That they may adorn the doctrine of God our Saviour in all things"* (verse 10).

Wuest translates it: *"embellish with honour the Word of God"*. In other words, when we serve faithfully we *"beautify the Bible"* and make the Christian message attractive to the lost.

These practical instructions given to old, to young, to men, to women and to slaves are interesting in view of the character of people on the island of Crete. Do you recall what they were like? *"Liars, evil beasts and lazy gluttons"* (Titus 1:12). But, the gospel changes people.

The great incentive to godly living is the Cross and the Coming, for undergirding these practical exhortations is:

(b) THE DOCTRINAL FOUNDATION
Verses 11-15

The emphasis here is on grace. Remember there were some who wanted to turn grace into licence. They were saying: *"We can live in sin because we are no longer under law"*, but grace brings an even greater responsibility.

Do you see here the three tenses of the Christian life in verses 11 to 13?

Past: *"The grace of God that bringeth salvation hath appeared to all men"*
Present: *"teaching us that"*
Future: *"looking for that blessed hope, and the glorious appearing"*

We are saved from the **Penalty of sin** (verse 11).
We are saved from the **Power of sin** (verse 12).
We are saved from the **Presence of sin** (verse 13).

Do you see here the three aspects of the Christian life in verse 12?

The Selfward Aspect: *"we should live soberly"*
The Manward Aspect: *"we are to live righteously"*
The Godward Aspect: *"we are to live godly"*

Notice also the teaching that the Lord's Advent is in two stages: *"That blessed hope"*, that is, the hope of meeting Christ in the air (1 Thessalonians 4:17).

"The glorious appearing", that is, the appearing of Christ with His church when He comes to the earth (2 Thessalonians 1:10).

Do you know what the great inspiration for godly living is? The Second Coming of Christ and the tremendous cost of Calvary. We look back to the Cross and we look forward to the Coming, and those twin truths motivate us to: *"live soberly, righteously and godly in this present world"*.

3. The Obligation of the Church
Chapter 3

Do you see how Paul puts this obligation to Titus? *"Put them in mind"* (verse 1). There are certain things Paul wants Titus to call to their attention and cause them to remember.

What are they? He wants them to remember they have an obligation to:

(a) THE STATE
Verses 1-8

When Paul penned these words, the Emperor at the time was Nero. His persecution of Christians is well-documented in history. Paul, however, is telling Titus to remind the Christians that they are to be subject to those powers, even though they are evil. They have to be: *"ready to every good work"* (verse 1).

A Christian is someone who is *"in the world but not of this world"* (John 17:14 and Philippians 3:20). However, Christians still live in the world and we ought to be good citizens. Of course, if the laws contradict the Word of God, our first allegiance is to the Lord (Acts 4:19 and Chapter 5:29).

The word: *"gentle"* in verse 2 means: *"sweet reasonableness"*. Paul is saying: *"Don't be too hard on these sinners around you. That is what you were like before you were saved!"*

"For we ourselves also were sometimes foolish, disobedient, deceived, serving divers lusts and pleasures, living in malice and envy, hateful, and hating one another" (verse 3).

In this verse, he talks about out *Past*.

In verses 4 and 5, he talks about our *Present*:

"But after that the kindness and love of God our Saviour toward man appeared, Not by works of righteousness which we have done, but

according to His mercy He saved us, by the washing of regeneration, and renewing of the Holy Ghost."

In verse 7, he talks about our *Future:*

"That being justified by His grace, we should be made heirs according to the hope of eternal life."

What a wonderful salvation is ours!

Do you not think it ought to motivate us to be better citizens so that the lost around us might see Christ in us?

(b) THE SCRIPTURES
Verses 9-11

"A man that is an heretick after the first and second admonition reject" (verse 10).

The Bible has a lot to say about discipline in the local church (Matthew 18:15-20 and 1 Corinthians 5:5). The word *"heretic"* suggests a person who causes division in the church because he forces people to decide or choose. *"Are you for me or for the elders?"* This is a work of the flesh (Galatians 5:20). Such a person should be admonished. It implies a public admonition, then a warning and then finally dismissed from the fellowship.

The elements in good church government are sound doctrine, sound discipleship and sound discipline.

(c) THE SERVANTS
Verses 12-15

What a blessing it is to have reliable colleagues!

Paul mentions four of them. He informs Titus that *"reinforcements are coming"* in the persons of *Artemas* or *Tychicus* for one of them was going to replace Titus. Is it not encouraging to know that when God moves a servant, He has a replacement ready to step in? It is possible that *Zenas* and *Apollos* carried this letter to Titus (Acts 18:24)

They were God's servants and Titus was to see that they had everything they needed. We should thank God for faithful servants. Faithful Sunday School teachers, faithful elders, faithful deacons and faithful preachers of the Word. But, do we do everything we can to help the Lord's servants?

Paul says: *"And let our people also learn to maintain good works to meet urgent needs that they may not be unfruitful"* (verse 14).

Do you want to be a faithful Christian? Do you want to be a fruitful Christian? Then, are you willing to stand by others who **Protect the Word (1 Timothy); Preach the Word (2 Timothy) and Practise the Word (Titus)**?

CHAPTER 18

Philemon

The ringing of the doorbell in the preacher's house in the middle of the night nearly wakened everyone in that home. Such calls were not unknown and they nearly always signalled trouble. The boyish voice of the speaker reminded the preacher of a week at Glorieta Baptist Assembly. *There he had met a boy from the distant city who had come along.* He was not a member of the church. Indeed, he was not a Christian. The preacher and the boy got to know each other through the Bible Study Class they shared. Many long conversations during the afternoons of that week helped the preacher know this lonely boy, at odds with this world, estranged from his family and groping to find his way in life. Those conversations also brought that boy to a realization of his need of Christ. It was a wonderful moment when that boy said: *"Yes!"* to the Lord and was gloriously saved.

Now he was calling, having just arrived in town with no place to stay. The boy had run away from home. He poured out the frustration of his soul, telling about the impossibility of getting through to his parents who could not accept his new found faith.

Problems were many and serious, but step by step the situation was faced. A call was made to the parents to calm their fears, and at last that boy was persuaded to board a bus for home. Mixed emotions swept through the preacher's heart as he watched the boy who was reluctant to go home, board that bus and return to his parents.

I wonder, what did Paul feel on the day when he watched Onesimus start back to Colosse and possibly return back to slavery? What ran through the mind of Onesimus, the runaway slave, as he started back to his master?

You see, Onesimus was a slave belonging to Philemon who had not only run away from his master but had probably stolen from him also (verse 18).

He ended up a distance of 1000 miles away among the throngs of the city of Rome where Paul was a prisoner. In some way, possibly because of conviction of sin, or fear of being found out, or through meeting Epaphras, then on visit to Rome from Colosse to see Paul, Onesimus came under the ministry of the imprisoned apostle.

That ministry bore great fruit. Paul led Onesimus to faith in Christ and became so fond of this new convert that he spoke of feeling for him as father would for his child (verse 10). So Paul now writes to Philemon requesting him to forgive Onesimus, to receive Onesimus, to recognize Onesimus not now as a slave but as *"a brother beloved"* (verse 16).

Is God's grace not amazing? Here was Onesimus, running away from Philemon, such a great distance to Rome, only to fall into the hands of Paul of all people, who led him to Christ.

Is this God of providence your God?
Is this God of power your God?
Is this God of patience your God?

Have you become discouraged because of the indifference of your unsaved family? Have you become disheartened because of their disinterest in the things of God?

Will you remember Onesimus who ran away from his master, only to run into his Saviour?

Although this letter is small in its quantity, it is not small in its quality. Here is a purely private letter, the only one that has been included in the Canon of Scripture. It expounds no doctrine. It exposes no error, but it exalts the Lord and encourages Christian courtesy in all circles of society. It is the shortest yet one of the sweetest of Paul's letters.

Now in order for us to see this letter in its historical context, we need to notice:

(1) The Locality of the Church

Do you see verses 1 and 2?

"Paul, a prisoner of Jesus Christ, and Timothy our brother, unto Philemon our dearly beloved, and fellowlabourer, And to our beloved Apphia, and Archippus our fellowsoldier, and to the church in thy house."

That second verse refers to: *"the church in thy house"*. Where was that? Well, if we compare this letter with Colossians, we discover that Philemon lived at Colosse (Colossians 4:9, 16-17). Now Colosse, as we have noted when studying Colossians, was one of a trio of cities - Hierapolis and Laodicea being the other two. It was located about 125 miles south east of the city of Ephesus. No doubt this church was the outgrowth of Paul's three year ministry at Ephesus (Acts 19, 20:17-18).

(2) The Slavery of the Empire

Onesimus was a slave (verse 16). Scholars tell us that there were 60 million slaves in the Roman Empire, men and women who were treated like pieces of merchandise to buy and sell. You see, a slave was not considered a person but a living tool. Any master had the right of life and death over his slaves. Pliny tells how Vedius Pollio treated a slave. The slave was carrying a tray of crystal goblets into the courtyard when he dropped and broke one. Immediately Pollio ordered the slave to be thrown into the fishpond in the middle of the courtyard where the man-eating fish tore him to pieces.

Slavery was an accepted institution in the Roman Empire. The question has often been posed: Why did Paul make no attempt to abolish slavery?

Actually, Paul had a tender interest in the welfare of slaves (1 Corinthians 7:20-24; Ephesians 6:5-9 and Colossians 3:22-4:1), but he recognized that salvation is better than legislation. *Getting laws right is good, but getting hearts right is even better.* Moreover, about two-thirds of the Roman Empire were slaves and to have argued for its abolition would have been to argue for chaos in society. Instead, Paul just broke slavery from the inside by changing relationships and attitudes involved.

This is seen in this very letter. Paul urges Philemon to see Onesimus as a brother not as a piece of property. He referred to Onesimus as: *"my son"* (verse 10) who is *"dear to me"* (verse 16).

Do you know why we do not have slavery in Western civilization today? It is because hearts and minds were changed by the Christian gospel and by Christian principles of human love, grace, and equality.

(3) The Adversity of the Apostle

Do you see how Paul begins this letter?

"Paul, a prisoner of Jesus Christ" (verse 1).

Paul wrote this little note about 62 A.D. during his first Roman imprisonment. This letter belongs to what we call the *"Prison Epistles"*, the others being Ephesians, Colossians and Philippians.

If we had been there, we might have had a conversation with Paul like this:
"Poor Paul, it is too bad these Romans put you in jail!"

Paul would have replied:
"They didn't put me in jail."

We would have said:
"Oh, we know what you mean. Those hateful religious rulers brought a charge against you"

Paul would have responded:
"They did not put me in jail either."

That would have confused us:
"Who put you in jail, then?"

Paul would have explained:
"Jesus Christ. I'm His prisoner."

That would have confused us further:
"You mean to tell me that you would serve Someone who would put you in prison?"

"Yes, when it is His will for me to be in prison, I'm in prison.
When it is His will for me to be out of prison, I'll be out of prison.
When it is His will for me to be sick, I'm going to be sick.
I belong to Him.
Since I belong to Him, I have learned to be content in whatsoever state I am.
Everything is all right.
Don't worry about me for 'we know that all things work together for good to them that love God.' (Romans 8:28)
Things are working together for my good and for God's glory."

What a man! A giant for God. Here was Paul in prison and he might have said: *"This is the end of my ministry"*, but he shuts his eyes to all secondary causes and sees in his imprisonment, as Joseph, long before, had seen in his, an all-wise providence.

Paul says: *"I am a prisoner, not of Nero, nor of Rome but of Jesus Christ for it is Christ who sent me to Rome"* (Acts 23:11).

You see:

1. Paul Recognised the Providence of God

It would have been easy for him to sulk and to quit his God, but Paul saw the Divine aspect of his trial.

Do *you* feel that you cannot get free from your situation? Are you depressed, frustrated, disillusioned? Do you need to look higher? Higher than the problem, higher than the pressure, higher than the persecution? Do you need to rise above your circumstances and fix your eyes on the God of providence? (Genesis 50:20) Do you see the providence of God in that situation in which you find yourself?

2. Paul Recognised the Purpose of God

There was the reduction of his movement, but there was the reach of his ministry.

While Paul was in prison, he *"redeemed the time"* (Ephesians 5:16). There was:

The Power of His Pen: Four New Testament letters flowed from his pen at this time.

The Power of His Prayers: Paul believed that prayer is effectual with God so he prayed much while he had the opportunity to do so (Ephesians 3:14; Philippians 1:9-11 and Colossians 1:9).

The Power of His Preaching: Is this not how Onesimus came to hear the gospel and believe on Christ?

"Paul, a prisoner of Jesus Christ."

Is this how you see yourself? Not physically, but spiritually. Are you a captive to the Lord's Will, the Lord's Word, the Lord's Work?

(4) The Intimacy of the Letter

This book, the shortest of all Paul's epistles, is one of four personal letters to individuals penned by Paul. The others are: 1 and 2 Timothy and Titus. I say this is an intimate letter because it deals with a delicate subject, forgiveness. The word: *"forgive"* means: *"to dismiss absolutely from one's thought"* (Exodus 34:6-7). Can you imagine Onesimus heading back to Colosse with this covering letter in his hand? Can you see him as he approaches Philemon's house? What was going through his mind?

> *Could Philemon forgive Onesimus?*
> *Should Philemon forgive Onesimus?*
> *Would Philemon forgive Onesiums?*

Well, look at what scholars call: ***"a literary gem"*** and notice:

1. The PREREQUISTE to FORGIVENESS
Verses 1-7

What is required before forgiveness can be expressed? Why, you must be forgiven - and there is abundant evidence here that Philemon was a true servant of the Lord. Can you see a beautiful picture of a Christian household here? Philemon, whose name means: *"affectionate"*, his wife Apphia and their son Archippus, who may have had pastoral oversight in the church, taking the place of Epaphras (Colossians 4:17) who had gone to Rome to help Paul (verse 23). You see:

(a) Philemon's Heart was Touched by God's Grace

Do you see how Paul describes Philemon in verse 1? *"Our dearly beloved, and fellow labourer."* It would be fascinating to know when, where, and how Philemon had first met Paul. Perhaps news of what was happening at Ephesus had reached Colosse. What was happening? To Ephesus had come a small wiry little Jew, a tentmaker by trade, an evangelist by calling. Paul had stayed in Ephesus for three whole years during which time all of Asia *"heard the Word"* (Acts 19:10). His preaching had turned Ephesus upside down and inside out. There was a great moving of the Holy Spirit. Multitudes had been converted to Jesus Christ (Acts 19:18-20). All kinds of miracles had been performed. A public bonfire of priceless books on the occult had been burned. *News of these startling happenings must have spread in all directions.*

No doubt Philemon had come to Ephesus to see for himself what was taking place, just as people, at the turn of the 20th Century, came from all over Britain to see what was happening in Wales at the time of the Welsh Revival.

However it came about, Philemon and Paul had met. It was truly a momentous meeting for verse 19 suggests that it was Paul who led Philemon to faith in Christ. Paul used this special relationship to encourage his friend to receive Onesimus. Christians, above all people, should be magnanimous, generous and sincere in forgiveness.

Has your heart been touched by the grace of God? Then you should be willing to forgive.

(b) Philemon's Hands were Touched by God's Grace

Paul refers to Philemon as: *"our dearly beloved, and fellow labourer"* or: *"fellow-worker"*. It would remind Philemon of the time during Paul's three year stint at Ephesus (Acts 20:31) when he helped the apostle in the work of the gospel. Philemon shared his faith. Do you? Do you know what it is to *"gossip the gospel"*?

(c) Philemon's Home was Touched by God's Grace

Paul speaks in verse 2 of: *"the church in thy house"*. First Century churches met in homes (Romans 16:5 and 1 Corinthians 16:19), church buildings being unknown until the Third Century. Here is a little company of believers meeting for worship in Philemon's home. I wonder, does the atmosphere of your home make it like a church?

One little boy was asked why he believed in God?
"Well", he replied, *"I guess it just runs in the family."*
That was, in a sense: *"the church in your house"*.
In contrast, the story is told of the pastor who visited a home.
The mother was very much concerned about making the proper impression.
 She called to her daughter: *"Honey, bring the book that mother loves so much and reads so often!"*
The little girl entered the room with the Sears catalogue!

But what a home this was. You see, Philemon:

Entertained the Saints

The church met in his house. Moreover, do you see how Paul closes the letter? He says: *"Prepare me also a lodging"* (verse 22). *"Philemon, get the guest room ready."* Paul anticipated that he would soon be released in response to the prayers of Philemon and others – and he wanted to visit him.

Have you ever thought about the hospitality commands of the New Testament? It ought to mark the pastor/elder: *"given to hospitality"* (1 Timothy 3:2). It ought to mark the believer: *"use hospitality one to another without grudging"* (1 Peter 4:9).

"A cold, unfriendly church contradicts the gospel message. Yet unfriendliness stands out as one of the most common criticisms people have of local churches." (Alexander Strauch)

It begs the question - Is *your* home open?

Encouraged the Saints

Paul says: *"The bowels (hearts) of the saints are refreshed by thee, brother"* (verse 7). The word: *"refreshed"* is from *"anapauo"*, a military term that speaks of an army resting from a march. Philemon was a second Barnabas, a true son of consolation, a son of encouragement. Everywhere he went, he had a word of encouragement for every believer and a helping hand for all who loved the Lord.

Have you discovered that some people when they come around you and talk with you, they depress you? When they are gone, you say: *"Well, thank goodness for that!"* They are fault finding, critical, so negative, hard and gloomy.

Then there are others and you are not in their company five minutes till a shot of sunshine has permeated your whole being. This was Philemon, forever the one to encourage, to refresh, to strengthen. Is this you?

Enriched the Saints

"That the communication of thy faith may become effectual by the acknowledging of every good thing which is in you in Christ Jesus" (verse 6).

The word translated: *"communication"* is better rendered: *"fellowship"*. Handley Moule suggests that the word, as used here, refers to Philemon's generous financial fellowship motivated by his love for the Saviour. I wonder, had Paul benefitted from Philemon's generosity? I wonder, was Epaphras in Rome because Philemon had sent him? (Colossians 4:12). Whatever, he saw his money as belonging to God (1 Chronicles 29:14). *Is that how you look upon your money?* You see, you will never put God ahead of money until you understand that your money is really His money. *If you want to know whether God is really first in your life, look at your cheque book. The rest is just talk.* Has God blessed you financially? (Deuteronomy 8:18) Well, are you using His money to further His cause?

What a man Philemon was, but he was about to face a serious test of his faith and love as he learned about the conversion of Onesimus. For notice here:

2. The PLEA for FORGIVENESS
Verses 8-16

Do you notice that Paul will not command but he will appeal? He will not hesitate to use every argument he can, even the argument of his age and bonds. You see, Paul is pleading on behalf of his son now and as he intercedes for Onesimus, he presents three strong appeals. In effect, he says: *"Philemon, recognize:"*

(a) THE POWER OF GOD

Onesimus is a Saved Man.

Do you see how Paul describes him in verse 10?

"Whom I have begotten in my bonds."

Think of this. *A free man came to Paul bound, a bound man left Paul free.* Onesimus was truly saved. The very fact that he had gone back to Colosse to *"face the music"* indicates that he was really saved. Debt dodging and duty dodging do not belong to the Christian faith. There is the need for apology and restitution. Salvation is free, but the moral obligations that accompany it can often prove to be very expensive indeed. Here was Onesimus, but he was not the Onesimus Philemon had previously known. He was a new man, for the Bible says: *"If any man be in Christ, he is a new creature: old things are passed away; behold, all things are become new"* (2 Corinthians 5:17).

Are you a new person? Have you shown the fruit of genuine repentance? Onesimus' material status was that of a mere slave, the lowest of the low. Yet his spiritual status was that of a child of God, the highest of the high.

Philemon and Onesimus were now brothers in the Lord. They now had the same Father, God the Father. They had both been redeemed by the same Saviour's precious blood. They were both indwelt by the same Holy Spirit.

Would it not be unthinkable for Philemon to turn away such a person?

Yet, perhaps, is that not what you are doing? Turning away your brother or sister?

The day we got saved we forfeited our rights in this matter of forgiveness. It really is not an option and in life we will be challenged when it comes to people who have done us wrong. It does not matter if we are right or wrong, but what matters is that we fully and freely extend Christian forgiveness.

If Philemon did not forgive Onesimus, then he would become the slave. He would be bound (Matthew 18:34). Are you bound? Do you need to be set free from internal torment that flows from an unforgiving spirit?

(b) THE PURPOSE OF GOD

Onesimus is a Serving Man.

Paul engages in a play on words here. You see, Onesimus was a common slave name, meaning: *"useful"*.

Paul says, in effect: *"Mr. Useful may have been Mr. Useless to you once, but now he's Mr. Useful once more!"*

Paul loved Onesimus and would have kept him in Rome as a fellow worker, but he did not want to tell Philemon what to do. Voluntary service and sacrifice motivated by love is what the Lord wants from His children.

Onesimus is now useful to the Lord. Is this not the purpose of God in conversion? That we live a purposeful, useful, and fruitful life. While we are most definitely saved by faith and not by works, true faith definitely works. Paul says: *"For we are His workmanship, created in Christ Jesus unto good works"* (Ephesians 2:10).

Do you know what we are saved *from*? Useless living.
Do you know what we are saved *by*? The grace of God.
Do you know what we are saved *for*? To glorify God and to enjoy Him forever.
Do you know how that is *done*? By purposeful, useful, fruitful lives.

(c) THE PROVIDENCE OF GOD

Onesimus is a Separated Man.

Do you see how Paul puts it in verse 15?

"For perhaps he therefore departed for a season, that thou shouldest receive him for ever."

"For perhaps" - because no man can see the secret providence of God at work, yet surely God had this in mind when Onesimus

fled? While *we* are unable to reconcile the sovereignty of God with the responsibility of man, we are forced to confess that *God Himself* can. The story of Onesimus and Philemon is a real life illustration of Romans 8 verse 28: *"And we know that all things work together for good to them that love God, to them who are the called according to His purpose"*.

I wonder, did Philemon really believe that God was working for his good when Onesimus had just robbed him and deserted him? Hardly, but unknown to Philemon, and unknown to you, God is in complete control.

He rules and overrules.

God permitted Onesimus to go to Rome that he might meet Paul and become a believer.

Monica, the mother of St. Augustine, pleads with God that her son might not go to Rome with all its temptations and debauchery, all its idolatry and immorality. Yet God in His providence allows him to go and there in that very place which has been dreaded by his mother Augustine is brought to a saving knowledge of the Lord Jesus.

How do we react when God allows a difficult trial to cross our pathway? How do we cope when a harsh providence comes our way? Can we take everything that happens to us as coming from the hand of God even when: *"God moves in a mysterious way, His wonders to perform"*? Do we look at the mystery of providence from an eternal standpoint?

God can bring blessing out of harsh circumstances.
God can bring good out of evil.
God bring joy out of despair.

Philemon could look back years later and say:

*"I'll bless the hand that guided,
I'll bless the heart that planned."*

3. The PRICE of FORGIVENESS
Verses 17-22

What about the money that Onesimus took? What about the Roman law that demanded branding or death? In those days, if you were a runaway slave and were caught, one of two things would happen. Either you would be killed or else you would be branded with the letter: "F" on your forehead. "F" for "Fugitive" – a runaway slave.

Can Onesimus go around smiling, as if to say: *"I sure am glad that everything has worked out so wonderfully!"*?

No!

We still have *an offender* in Onesimus and *the offended* in Philemon. Therefore, something must be done. The debt must be paid. Somehow, the account is going to have be settled. It is here that Paul's statement becomes so precious: *"If he hath wronged thee, or oweth thee aught, put that on mine account"* (verse 18).

Is this not a marvellous picture of the work of Christ? Is this not a wonderful illustration of how our account is settled with an offended God? You know, when we think of an account, we usually think of:

(a) STARTING THE ACCOUNT

Most of us are familiar with an account of some kind. But, whether it is a credit card account, or a bank account, the account has to be started.

Do you know something? Man does not go through life without an account with God. That account was opened in the Garden of Eden. Just as everything was going well until Onesimus wronged Philemon, thus starting his account, so everything was fine until Adam wronged God with his sin. Then, the account was opened for all of us, the offspring of Adam.

Paul says:

"Wherefore, as by one man sin entered into the world, and death by sin; and so death passed upon all men, for that all have sinned" (Romans 5:12).

Our sins, offences, wrongs: they must all be paid for. That brings us to think of:

(b) SETTLING THE ACCOUNT

Paul says: *"Look, if Onesimus stole something from you, just put it on my account. Put it on my credit card"* (verse 18).

Dr. Scofield puts it like this:

"'Receive him as myself' (verse 17) - reckon to him my merit. 'If he hath wronged thee, or oweth thee ought, put that on mine account' (verse 18) - reckon to me his demerit."

Is this not the glory of the gospel? It is as though we hear Christ say to the Father: *"Father, put that on Mine account!"* But do not stop there, for there is more. His clean account, His righteousness, has been imputed to us.

Our account becomes His. His account becomes ours.

Both of these truths are incorporated in one of the most wonderful verses in the Bible:

"For He hath made Him to be sin for us, who knew no sin; that we might be made the righteousness of God in Him" (2 Corinthians 5:21).

Bible scholars call this: *"the doctrine of imputation"*. Our sins were imputed to Christ, charged to His account. Likewise, because of Calvary, Christ's righteousness is credited to our account putting us *"in the black"* with God.

Do not forget that Paul is writing this note to plead with Philemon to forgive, to receive, to restore Onesimus. It is as though Paul is saying to Philemon: *"Freely ye have received, freely give"* (Matthew 10:8). Indeed, when writing to the Colossian church which met in Philemon's home, Paul says: *"Forgiving one another .... even as Christ forgave you, so also do ye"* (Colossians 3:13).

Here is where *"the rubber hits the road"*. In spite of all we did to God, He forgave us. Therefore, we ought to forgive others. Have you been deeply hurt by a fellow believer? Do you find forgiveness difficult? Do you need to stand under the shadow of the Cross and think about God's free forgiveness of your sins there? Having received His eternal forgiveness, how can you not extend temporal forgiveness?

Charles Spurgeon said: ***"Go to Calvary to learn how you may be forgiven and then linger there to learn how to forgive!"***

4. The PARTNERS in FORGIVENESS
Verses 23-25

The Christian life is not lived in a vacuum. Believers do not act alone, independent of the fellowship. By sending greetings from five men known to him, Paul reminds Philemon of his accountability to them all. Failure to forgive Onesimus would disappoint their high expectations of him, and bring him under their discipline.

Look at them briefly. When we think of:

(a) Epaphras: we think of Fellowship

Paul says: *"Epaphras, my fellow-prisoner"* (verse 23). Was he the pastor / teacher of the church that met in Philemon's home? (Colossians 1:7 and Chapter 4:12) But now he was identified closely with Paul in the apostle's imprisonment. You see, fellowship is identifying the needs of others and seeking to minister to those needs.

(b) Marcus: we think of Failure

John Mark got *"cold feet"* on Paul's first missionary journey and went home to his mother (Acts 13:13). But, is it not wonderful to know that *failure is not final.* Such is the restoring grace of God that Mark the failure made good and came to spiritual maturity (2 Timothy 4:11).

Do you feel that you are a failure? Have you let the Lord down? Have you let others down? Like Mark, do you need to pray: *"Lord, restore unto me the joy of Thy salvation"?* (Psalm 51:12)

(c) Aristarchus: we think of Faithfulness

A native of Thessalonica (Acts 20:4 and Chapter 27:2), he had a long association with Paul and had been through some rough times with him (Acts 19:29 and Chapter 27:4). He was Paul's fellow-worker, Paul's fellow-prisoner (Colossians 4:10). Indeed, according to tradition, Aristarchus was martyred in Rome during the persecutions under Nero. Here was a man who was faithful to Paul through thick and thin.

Do you need a model for what it is to be a friend? Then Aristarchus is your man.

(d) Demas: we think of Folly

He is described here as one of Paul's fellow workers, but later we read: *"Demas hath forsaken me, having loved this present world"* (2 Timothy 4:10). He began well, but he did not last.

Do you know someone who began well but the temptations of this world proved to be too strong? Do you know someone who once attended most faithfully but for various reasons fell away? What a warning Demas is! *"Wherefore let him that thinketh he standeth take heed lest he fall"* (1 Corinthians 10:12).

Finally:

(e) Luke: we think of Fellow-Feeling

Sympathy! Luke, *"the beloved physican"* (Colossians 4:14), was a

Gentile Christian doctor and the author of the third Gospel and the Acts. He was a frequent travelling companion of Paul and no doubt took care of the apostle's physical needs (2 Corinthians 12:7). Just before his martyrdom, Paul said: *"Only Luke is with me"* (2 Timothy 4:11).

What a man, bearing Paul's burdens, with him to the very end. Do we know what it is to: *"Bear ... one another's burdens, and so fulfil the law of Christ"*? (Galatians 6:2)

Now these five men were known to Philemon. He had the opportunity to set a good example for them by forgiving Onesimus. On the other hand, failing to forgive would fracture the bond of fellowship Philemon enjoyed with them.

Now the book of Philemon ends here, but not the story. How did it end? Did Philemon forgive Onesimus?

It is probable that he not only forgave him but that he freed him (verse 21). It is unlikely that this book would have found its way into the New Testament canon if he had not.

Carla Barton, the founder of the American Red Cross, was once painfully betrayed by a fellow worker. Years later a friend reminded her of the incident.
"I don't remember that", replied Miss Barton.
"You don't remember?" asked the astonished friend. *"But you were so hurt at the time. Surely you must remember."*
"No", Clara insisted gently.
"I distinctly remember forgetting it ever happened."

Do you need to extend forgiveness to someone? Have you been nursing a grudge? Are you giving someone the silent treatment? Are you not ready to forgive the debt?

How can you sit at the Lord's Supper with an unforgiving spirit? How can you sit there and think about God forgiving you, when you will not forgive others?

Your unwillingness to forgive is unthinkable. It is a rebellious, blatant, open act of disobedience to God, for we are to forgive others as God has forgiven us (Ephesians 4:32 and Colossians 3:13).

Philemon forgave his Onesimus.

Is it not time that you forgave yours?

CHAPTER 19
Hebrews

When it comes to the book of Hebrews, opinions are divided!

Some Christians find it one of the most *difficult* books of the Bible. Hebrews is a tremendous book, but it is difficult to understand. This is partly due to the fact that to Gentile eyes it is a very Jewish letter describing sacrifices, altars and priests. To get a proper understanding of the book of Hebrews, we need to be familiar with the Old Testament, especially the book of Leviticus. Dr. Charles L. Feinberg said that you cannot understand the book of Hebrews unless you understand the book of Leviticus, because Hebrews is based on the principles of the Levitical priesthood.

Of course, there are others who find the book of Hebrews *delightful.* They like it because of the magnificent chapter on faith or because of the light it throws on the person, work and present ministry of the Lord Jesus Christ.

So, some think this book is difficult. Others think it is delightful.

Perhaps we should ask several questions as we come to this book.

Why was this letter written?
Who was its author?
To whom was this letter sent?
When was it sent?

Now those are maybe straightforward questions but the answers are not!

A Journey Through The Bible

Let us think for a moment about:

1. The Diverse People

The oldest and most reliable manuscripts refer to this book simply as: *"To the Hebrews"*. The Hebrews, the Jews, were and are a people like no other people. Do you recall what Paul said when speaking of Israel? *"To whom pertaineth the adoption, and the glory, and the covenants, and the giving of the law, and the service of God, and the promises; whose are the fathers"* (Romans 9:4-5).

These people, the Hebrews, were inheritors of a wonderful past and of a God-given revelation. They had the Law, the Covenants, the Tabernacle, the Temple and the Sacrifices. They had Abraham and Moses and Samuel and David and a long line of prophets, priests and kings.

But now, some of these Jews had embraced Christianity and were being taunted by the Jews as apostates from Jehovah, as renegades from Moses, as abandoning their law, and as forfeiting all the blessings and promises of the Old Covenant to become the followers of a crucified malefactor.

You see, this book was probably written to Jewish believers before the destruction of the Temple by Titus in A.D. 70. Hebrews 10 verse 11 infers that the Temple system was still in operation and some scholars think it was written about A.D. 64.

But where was this letter sent to? The only address on it is: *"To the Hebrews"*. Well, you can take your pick! Some say it was sent to Alexandria or Ephesus or Antioch or Jerusalem. Wherever it was, here was a letter addressed to Hebrew Christians, to some particular Jewish group or church who were long established (Hebrews 5:12) and who were well acquainted with the Old Testament Scriptures. Jewish believers who were now under intense pressure to *repudiate Christ* and to *return* to the *Temple* and all the ritual of Judaism (Hebrews 10:32-34).

Nero was now on the imperial throne and Nero's reign was a

94

time of great persecution for the church. These Jewish Christians had steadfastly endured such persecution but now they were in danger of drifting from their Christian faith back to the ritual of Judaism. You see, the Jews had a way of escape from suffering that was not open to Gentile believers. The Jewish believers could get out of persecution by going back to the synagogue. As David Pawson points out: *"At this time Christianity was illegal, but Judaism was still legal"*. So there was a way out of persecution. They could go back to the Jewish ritual. They could return to the synagogue but in so doing they would have to say: *"I deny that Jesus Christ is the Messiah"*.

So can you see now:

2. The Definite Purpose

The writer calls this epistle: *"the word of exhortation"* (Hebrews 13:22). The Greek word translated: *"exhortation"* simply means: *"encouragement"*. According to the *Oxford English Dictionary*, the word: *"exhort"* means: *"to admonish urgently, to urge someone to a course of action"*.

The writer of Hebrews says in the first verse of Chapter 6: *"Let us go on unto perfection"*. The idea is of going on to spiritual maturity. The appeal is: *"Please don't go back, but do go on!"*

Someone died in the caves and potholes of Yorkshire. This is what the coroner said at the inquest: *"If he had just kept moving, he would be alive today"*. Instead he sat down and stayed in one place and hypothermia set in.

Is this not one of the main themes of the Book of Hebrews? *"Keep moving!"*

Go through the book of Hebrews and discover how many times that little phrase: *"Let us"* appears.

Indeed, there are many key expressions which run throughout this epistle that bring out the main purpose. One such key word is *"perfection"* or *"perfect"* used fourteen times. It is not the idea of *"sinlessness"*. Rather, it is contrasting the mature Christian experience with the immature one (Hebrews 2:10 and Chapter 5:9).

The word: *"eternal"* or *"forever"* is used fifteen times to show that Christianity is a permanent reality, in contrast with Judaism which was temporary and passing (Hebrews 1:8; Chapter 5:6 and 9; Chapter 6:2 and Chapter 9:12).

A most important word is the word: *"better"*, used thirteen times in the book as the writer shows the superiority of Jesus Christ and His salvation over the Hebrew system of religion. We have a better persuasion (Hebrews 6:9); a better priesthood (Hebrews 7:7); a better hope (Hebrews 7:19); a better covenant (Hebrews 7:22); better promises (Hebrews 8:6); better sacrifices (Hebrews 9:23); a better reward (Hebrews 10:34); a better country (Hebrews 11:16) and a better resurrection (Hebrews 11:35).

Do you see what the writer wants his readers to grasp? He wants his fellow Jewish believers to see that in Christ they gained much more than they renounced in Judaism. Christianity is not supplementary to Judaism but it completely substitutes it, having in every way superseded it.

Consider for a moment:

3. The Difficult Passages

There are five warning passages in the book of Hebrews and much of the controversy which surrounds this letter is centred in them. Each of these passages encourages us to heed God's Word by pointing out the sad spiritual consequences that result if we do not.

Harold Willmington sets them out like this:

First Warning: Hebrews 2:1-4 - Disregarding God's Word
Second Warning: Hebrews 3:7-19 - Doubting God's Word

Third Warning: Hebrews 5:11-6:20 - Departing from God's Word
Fourth Warning: Hebrews 10:26-31 - Despising God's Word
Fifth Warning: Hebrews 12:25 - Disagreeing with God's Word

The third warning is found within a difficult passage that has upset many Christians, especially those who feel they have failed the Lord. Look at Chapter 6 verses 4 to 6:

"For it is impossible for those who were once enlightened, and have tasted of the heavenly gift, and were made partakers of the Holy Ghost, And have tasted the good word of God, and the powers of the world to come, If they shall fall away, to renew them again unto repentance; seeing they crucify to themselves the Son of God afresh, and put Him to an open shame."

This much debated passage has been understood in various ways.

Some hold that the people described in these verses are Christians who actually lose their salvation.

Some hold that these were Jewish unbelievers convinced of the truth but still uncommitted. People who came into contact with the gospel but were spiritually unchanged by it.

But look at the passage again and notice the words: *"they"* and *"them"*.

Dr. Sidlow Baxter says:

"The words refer exclusively to a special class, in special circumstances at a special historical crisis point which has forever passed away."

The tenth chapter of this book throws some light on the problem. Look for a moment at Chapter 10 verses 38 and 39:

"Now the just shall live by faith: but if any man draw back, My soul shall have no pleasure in him. But we are not of them who draw back unto perdition; but of them that believe to the saving of the soul."

Notice the word: *"we"*. It is emphatic and differentiates between true believers and empty professors. Here is something true Christians cannot do: *"If any man draw back"*, that is, if any man will give up Christ and return to the Old Testament ritual, *"My soul shall have no pleasure in him"*. Empty professors may draw back, but, says the writer, *"we are not of them who draw back unto perdition; but of them that believe to the saving of the soul."*

Alan Cairns says:

"Now that is the key to understanding the warning of chapter 6 and 10. Remember that it was written to Jews who were tempted to give up Christ. The sin that Paul is constantly dealing with in the book of Hebrews is not just any sin. It is the sin of repudiating Christ. That is the sin of the Book of Hebrews."

A true believer will never give up on Christ but empty professors will. Let no sincere Christian ever think for one moment that anything in the Hebrew letter contradicts that glorious guarantee of eternal security in Romans 8. Those who make this passage mean that a believer can lose his salvation will have to admit that it would then also make the point that they could never get it back again. But there is no possibility of a true Christian losing salvation. You see, our salvation is an eternal salvation.

The Lord Jesus says:

"And I give unto them eternal life; and they shall never perish, neither shall any man pluck them out of My hand" (John 10:28. See also Romans 8:35-39, Philippians 1:6 and 1 Peter 1:4-5).

> **"Once in Christ, in Christ forever,**
> **Nothing from His love can sever."**

4. The Different Penmen

Who wrote this letter to these Jewish believers?

Well, there have been all sorts of guesses. Tertullian of Carthage in the Third Century declared that *Barnabas* wrote it. Barnabas was a Levite and the book of Hebrews may have been written by a Levite. Others think that *Apollos* wrote it. Some think that *Luke* was the author.

I am inclined to believe that it was *Paul*. You see, Peter states that Paul wrote to the same people that he wrote to, that is Jews of the dispersion. Peter calls Paul's letter: *"Scripture"* (2 Peter 3:15-16). The only writing in Scripture that is addressed to Jews and is not credited to another author is Hebrews. Would that not make you think that Paul wrote this book?

But what about:

5. The Divine Person

It is this letter that exalts the person and work of the Lord Jesus. The book of Hebrews has been called: *"the fifth Gospel"*. The first four describe what Christ did on earth, while Hebrews describes what He is now doing in Heaven.

I want us to consider this book in three ways:

(1) A SUPERIOR PERSON
Chapter 1 - Chapter 4

Keep in mind that Paul is pleading with these Jewish believers not to go back to the past. His argument is very simple. It would be like this: You are riding in a Rolls-Royce. Now do you want to go back to driving an old banger? A photograph of a person can be helpful but it is unnecessary when the person is present himself. So with the Lord Jesus. Old Testament *"shadow"* is replaced by New Testament *"substance"*. *"Type"* is replaced by *"antitype"*. The Jewish faith has been superseded by the Christian faith. So Paul argues that having the Son of God is so many times better than having the servants of God.

You see:

(a) *Christis Superior to the Prophets*
Chapter 1 verses 1-3

These men who were held in the highest esteem by the Jewish people were called to be servants but Jesus Christ is the Son of God. They were spokesmen for God, but He is God speaking.

The point is made:

Jesus Christ is God's Final Revelation

Do you see how the letter opens?

"God, who at sundry times and in divers manners spake in time past unto the fathers by the prophets, hath in these last days spoken unto us by His Son" (Hebrews 1:1-2).

In the past, God had given His Word to the prophets in many instalments and by various methods. These revelations pointed to Christ and He is the final revelation from God. Christ is God's *"last Word"* to the world, for through Christ the heart, mind and will of God was made known.

"This is My beloved Son ... hear ye Him" (Matthew 17:5) was the message from God on the Mountain of Transfiguration. There are some people today who boast of having *"a new revelation"* from God. They are deceived, for God is not giving new revelations today. He is illuminating His once-for-all revelation in Christ.

Jesus Christ is God's Full Revelation

Can you see here **His Person**?

"His Son!" This implies sameness of essence with the Father. The Lord Jesus Himself said in John 10 verse 30: *"I and My Father are one"*.

"Who being the brightness of His glory, and the express image of His person, and upholding all things by the word of His power, when He had by Himself purged our sins, sat down on the right hand of the Majesty on high" (verse 3).

The expression: *"And the express image of His person,"* literally means that Jesus Christ is the *"exact representation of the very substance of God"*. Only He could honestly say: *"he that hath seen Me hath seen the Father"* (John 14:9).

Can you see here **His Power**?

Do you see how Christ stands in relation to the universe?

> He is its Creator – verse 2.
> He is its Possessor: *"heir of all things"*- verse 2.
> He is its Sustainer – verse 3.

The reason the universe is a cosmos and not chaos is because of the upholding power of Christ.

Are you doubting the ability of Christ to keep you? He is: *"able to keep you from falling"* (Jude 24).

Are you doubting the ability of Christ to strengthen you? He is: *"able to make all grace abound toward you"* (2 Corinthians 9:8).

Are you doubting the ability of Christ to answer your prayer? He is: *"able to do exceeding abundantly above all that we ask or think"* (Ephesians 3:20).

Can you see **His Passion**?

"When He had by Himself purged our sins."
Do you see the contrast?

> His person, His power …. our sins!
> It was His Cross, it was my sin.
> It was my sin, it was His Cross.

(b) *Christ is Superior to the Angels*
    Chapter 1 verse 4 to Chapter 2 verse 18

Angels played a vital role in the Jewish religion. Did you know that the law was given through the ministry of angels? (Acts 7:53 and Galatians 3:19) But Jesus Christ is far above angels.

He is the Son, they are but servants (Hebrews 1:5-9).

He is the Sovereign, they are but subjects (Hebrews 1:13-14).

Christ is superior to angels:

- in Sonship – verse 2
- in Heirship – verse 2
- in Kingship – verse 3
- in Worship – verse 6
- in Rulership – verse 13

Our trust then is not in angels but in Christ *"who displays superior power and guardian grace"*.

(c) *Christ is Superior to Moses*
    Chapter 3 verses 1-19

Moses was generally regarded by the Jews as one of their greatest leaders, but Jesus Christ is even greater. Do you recall that on the Mount of Transfiguration Christ meets with Moses and Elijah but He is clearly the superior one. The Father says: *"This is My beloved Son, in whom I am well pleased; hear ye Him"* (Matthew 17:5).

Moses was a servant; Christ is the Son.

Moses served in the house, while Christ is Lord over the house.

Moses ministered using symbols, while Christ is the fulfilment of those symbols.

How could these people go back to Judaism when what Christ offered was so much greater than what Moses could offer?

(d) Christ is Superior to Joshua
Chapter 4 verses 1-13

Joshua brought the children of Israel into a temporal rest, but Christ brings us into an eternal rest.

The Greek word for *"rest"* is used twelve times in Chapter 4, but not always with the same meaning.

There is *Creation Rest* (Genesis 2:2 and Hebrews 4:4)
There is *Canaan Rest* (Hebrews 3:11 and Chapter 4:5)
There is *Calvary Rest* (Hebrews 4:3, 10)
There is *Conquering Rest* (Hebrews 4:11) - the overcomer's present rest of victory.
There is *Complete Rest:* the future eternal rest in heaven (Hebrews 4:9)

This Chapter also records the first of thirteen *"Let us"* admonitions to be found in the book of Hebrews. Do you see them?

"Let us therefore fear" (Hebrews 4:1).
"Let us labour therefore" (Hebrews 4:11).
"Let us hold fast our profession" (Hebrews 4:14).
"Let us therefore come boldly unto the throne of grace" (Hebrews 4:16).

The others are Hebrews 6:1; 10:22; 10:23; 10:24; 12:1; 12:1; 12:28; 13:13 and 13:15.

But the point is this, *Christ is Superior to Joshua*.

(e) Christ is Superior to Aaron
Chapter 4 verses 14-16

Aaron ministered in an earthly tabernacle, but Christ our great high priest has passed into the heavens (Hebrews 4:14).

Aaron served for a few years, but the Lord Jesus is a priest forever after the order of Melchisedec (Hebrews 5:6).

The Aaronic priesthood was subject to death, but Christ ever liveth to make intercession (Hebrews 7:23, 25).

The sacrifices of the old order were offered up continuously, but Christ offered up Himself once for all (Hebrews 10:11-12).

Now do not forget Paul's objective! It is to show us the superiority of Jesus Christ. He is superior to the prophets, to the angels, to Moses, to Joshua and to Aaron. There were many stars of great magnitude in the Hebrew sky but the Lord Jesus outshines them all. So why go back to the inferior?

A Superior Person.

We can search literature and lexicons, histories and homilies, dictionaries and declarations only to discover:

> *"No mortal can with Him compare*
> *Among the sons of men;*
> *Fairer is He than all the fair,*
> *That fill the heavenly train."*

(2) A SUPERIOR PRIESTHOOD
Chapter 5 - Chapter 10

In the Old Testament, there are many *"shadows"* or *"types"* of the Lord Jesus. In this letter, there are twenty nine quotations from the Old Testament and fifty three direct allusions to the Old Testament. You see, the purpose of this letter is to show that the Old Testament revelation is fulfilled in the person and work of Jesus Christ. Here Paul is telling us that substance is better than shadows. He does that by introducing us to the priesthood.

Now, priests had great value in the Hebrew culture. We might ask: *"Well, what was a priest?"* When we were studying the book of Leviticus, we discovered that the term *"priest"* means: *"one who officiates"*. A prophet was someone who represented God to the people; a priest was someone who represented the people to God.

"Leviticus" means: *"pertaining to the Levites the priests"*. You see, if you were going to function in the priestly office, you had to be a Levite (Exodus 28:1 and Numbers 3:6). But now the writer to the Hebrews introduces a superior priesthood.

He says we have:

(a) A BETTER SAVIOUR
Chapter 5 - Chapter 6

Look at Chapter 5 verse 5:

"So also Christ glorified not Himself to be made an high priest; but He that said unto Him, Thou art My Son, to day have I begotten Thee."

Christ was not appointed by man; He was appointed by God,
Aaron was from the tribe of Levi; Jesus Christ was the Son of God.
Aaron had compassion, but Christ had greater sympathy.
Aaron offered animal sacrifices; the Lord Jesus offered Himself.
Aaron had to offer sacrifices for himself and his family. Not so with Jesus Christ. Being the sinless Lamb of God, He needed no sacrifices for sin.

A Better Saviour!

A great high priest who:

knows your trials –

"Who in the days of His flesh, when He had offered up prayers and supplications with strong crying and tears unto Him that was able to save Him from death, and was heard in that He feared; Though He were a Son, yet learned He obedience by the things which He suffered" (Hebrews 5:7-8).

feels your heartaches –

"For we have not an high priest which cannot be touched with the feeling of our infirmities; but was in all points tempted like as we are, yet without sin" (Hebrews 4:15).

and strengthens your soul –

"Let us therefore come boldly unto the throne of grace, that we may obtain mercy, and find grace to help in time of need" (Hebrews 4:16).

"Grace to help in the nick of time!"

**"Is there anyone can help us,
One who understands our hearts,
When the thorns of life have pierced them till they bleed?
One who sympathises with us,
Who in wondrous love imparts,
Just the very, very blessing that we need?**

**Yes, there's One, only One
The blessed Jesus, blessed Jesus, He's the One,
When afflictions press the soul,
When waves of trouble roll,
And you need a friend to help you,
He's the One."**

(b) A BETTER SOURCE
Chapter 7

Chapter 6 closes with these words:

"Jesus, made an high priest for ever after the order of Melchisedec."

Now, who was this mysterious Melchisedec?

Well, he is a type of Christ in *His Office*. He was both king and priest (Hebrews 7:2-3).

He is a type of Christ in *His Origin*. The Bible contains no record of his birth or death (Hebrews 7:3).

Melchisedec was a royal priest whose order took precedence over that of Aaron. Do you what that means? It means that Christ's priesthood is *timeless* (verse 3). Aaron and his sons died but Christ lives forever.

"But this man, because He continueth ever, hath an unchangeable priesthood" (verse 24).

His is an *everlasting* (verse 17), *unchanging* (verse 24) and *holy* priesthood (verse 26).

Is this not the high priest we need? There is no need to look beyond Jesus Christ. He is all that we need for time and for eternity. When we got Christ, we got it all!

(c) A BETTER SCRIPT
Chapter 8

Why go back to the Old Covenant now that you are in the New?

The *Old Covenant* was mediated by Moses (Hebrews 8:5); the *New Covenant* is mediated by Christ (Hebrews 8:6).

The *Old Covenant* was conditional (Deuteronomy 28:1 and Hebrews 8:9); the *New Covenant* is unconditional (Hebrews 8:10).

The *Old Covenant* could not produce the necessary righteousness (Hebrews 8:8); the *New Covenant* can produce the necessary righteousness (Hebrews 8:11).

The *Old Covenant* was written on dead stones (Exodus 32:15); the *New Covenant* is written on living hearts (Hebrews 8:10).

When did this New Covenant come into being? When Christ shed His blood on the Cross (Luke 22:20 and 1 Corinthians 11:23-26).

"Christ", says our author, *"is the mediator of a better covenant established upon better promises"* (Hebrews 8:6).

The question might be posed:

"Did Jeremiah not say that God promised this New Covenant to the Jews? (Jeremiah 31:31)? What right do we have to apply it to the church?"

Well, there are *prophetic elements* in this covenant which will be fulfilled with Israel and there are *salvation clauses* in this covenant into which the church enters today.

(d) A BETTER SANCTUARY
Chapter 9

The contrast is between the earthly and the heavenly. There was a sanctuary in the Old Testament. Indeed, there were two of them. First the tabernacle and then the temple, but both were *inaccessible* to the people (Hebrews 9:6-7) and both were *temporary* (Hebrews 9:8).

How different is this better sanctuary!

Do you see how the writer describes it?

"But Christ being come an high priest of good things to come, by a greater and more perfect tabernacle, not made with hands, that is to say, not of this building; Neither by the blood of goats and calves, but by His own blood He entered in once into the holy place, having obtained eternal redemption for us" (verses 11-12).

Through Christ we have access to that true tabernacle in Heaven.

(e) A BETTER SACRIFICE
Chapter 9 verse 13 – Chapter 10

Hundreds of thousands of animals were sacrificed in Old Testament times. Jewish altars ran with rivers of blood. But, it was not possible that the blood of bulls and goats could take away sin.

Those sacrifices could cover sin but they could never cleanse sin.

Christ's sacrifice takes away sin.

"And every priest standeth daily ministering and offering oftentimes the same sacrifices, which can never take away sins: But this man, after He had offered one sacrifice for sins for ever, sat down on the right hand of God; From henceforth expecting till His enemies be made His footstool.

For by one offering He hath perfected for ever them that are sanctified" (Hebrews 10:11-14).

Christ's sacrifice never needs to be repeated.

Well do we sing the words of Isaac Watts:

> *"Not all the blood of beasts*
> *On Jewish altars slain,*
> *Could give the guilty conscience peace*
> *Or wash away the stain.*
>
> *But Christ the heav'nly Lamb,*
> *Takes all our sins away;*
> *A sacrifice of nobler name,*
> *And richer blood than they."*

Calvary covers it all!

> *"Calvary covers it all,*
> *My past with its sin and stain,*
> *My guilt and despair,*
> *Jesus took on Him there,*
> *And Calvary covers it all!"*

So why go back to dead ritual?

(3) A SUPERIOR PRINCIPLE
Chapter 11 – Chapter 13

The principle is - *Faith.*

The fact that Christ is a superior person and that He exercises a superior priesthood ought to encourage us to put our trust in Him.

Indeed, almost the last verse of Chapter 10 says: *"the just shall live by faith"* (verse 38). But what is faith? The first verse of Chapter 11 tells us what faith is like:

"Now faith is the substance of things hoped for, the evidence of things not seen."

The word *"faith"* is the Greek word: *"pistis"* which means: *"belief, trust, confidence"*. The word *"substance"* means: *"assurance"* and *"evidence"* means: *"proof"*.

So, when the Holy Spirit gives us faith through the Word the very presence of faith in our hearts is all the assurance and evidence we need.

J. Oswald Sanders says:

"Faith enables the believing soul to treat the future as present and the invisible as seen."

All of us enjoy things by faith. Have you ever enjoyed a holiday in January even though you did not leave until July? You pictured yourself by the pool soaking up the sun. Have you ever done that?

By faith we enjoy in the present what is a future reality.

Well, that is what the writer is saying. Faith is making a present substance out of a future reality.

Warren Wiersbe says:

"True Bible faith is confident obedience to God's Word in spite of circumstances and consequences."

Martin Luther said:

"Faith sees the invisible, believes the incredible and receives the impossible. Then, it accepts the impossible, does without the indispensable and bears the intolerable."

Now the best way to grow in faith is to feed on the Word and walk with the faithful, for here we notice:

(a) THE PEOPLE OF FAITH
Chapter 11

Here the writer is presenting the roll call of faith.

As you read this wonderful Chapter that lists the heroes of faith, you discover that faith anticipates the future, acts in the present, evaluates the past, dares to move out and persists to the end.

When Hudson Taylor, the famous missionary, first went to China, it was in a sailing vessel. Very close to the shore of cannibal islands, the ship was caught in a windless calm, and was slowly drifting toward the shore. The savages were eagerly anticipating a feast.

The captain came to Mr. Taylor and asked him to pray for the help of God.

"I will", said Taylor, "provided you set your sails to catch the breeze".

The Captain declined to make himself a laughing stock by unfurling the sails in a dead calm. Taylor said: "I will not undertake to pray for the vessel unless you will prepare the sails to catch the wind when God sends it".

The captain set the sails.

While Taylor was engaged in prayer, there was a knock at the door of his room.

"Who is there?" Taylor asked.

The captain's voice responded: "Are you still praying for the wind?"

"Yes!" replied Hudson Taylor.

"Well", said the captain, "you better stop praying, for we have more wind than we can manage".

Charles Wesley wrote:

> "Faith, mighty faith, the promise sees,
> And looks to God alone;
> Laughs at impossibilities,
> And cries it shall be done."

(b) THE PATTERN OF FAITH
Chapter 12

Look to the Son of God (verses 1-3) and Submit to the Discipline of God (verses 4-11).

"Looking unto Jesus" (verse 2).

The phrase here speaks of a steadfast, intent and continuous gaze. In the Greek, it literally reads: *"Look away to Jesus"*.

When I am teaching my grandchildren how to kick a football, I constantly say to them: *"Keep your eye on the ball"*.

How easy it is to get our eyes off Christ and onto others. Keep your eyes on Christ. Why? Because He is the perfect model, the perfect example and the perfect pattern.

Someone has said that if you look outward you will be distressed, if you look inward you will be depressed, but if you look upward you will be blessed.

(c) THE PERFORMANCE OF FAITH
Chapter 13

Faith in relation to *Love* – verses 1-6.
Faith in relation to *Leadership* - *verses* 7, 17-19, 22-25.
Faith in relation to *Legalism* – *verses* 9-11,
Faith in relation to *Lordship* – verses 8, 12-16, 20-21.

Remember that in turning to Christ, these Hebrews lost the temple and its priesthood and sacrifices, but they gained in Christ far more than they lost.

They were being tempted to go back to Judaism and Paul cries:

"No! Instead of going back, go outside the camp and bear reproach and rejection with Christ."

"Why stay in Jerusalem when it is not your city? Jerusalem is doomed. Get out of the Jewish religious system and identify with the Saviour who died for you."

There can be no room for compromise.

Is this not what Polycarp (70-155 A.D.) did? See him in the Colosseum of Rome with the voice of the Emperor ringing out: *"Polycarp, renounce your Christ, or you shall die!"*
Hear him respond: *"Caesar, accept my Christ and you shall live!"*

See Martin Luther at the Council of Worms standing before the most powerful force of his day, the Roman Catholic Church, refusing to deny his faith:
"Here I stand. I can do no other. God help me."

See John Bunyan in a loathsome prison declaring:
"I am determined, God being my helper and shield, to stay here until the moss grows over my eyebrows rather than surrender my faith."

Is this not exactly what these Jewish Christians were being tempted to do? To give up Christ and return to the Jewish ritual. Could it be that you are drifting spiritually?

Do you need to be reminded of the truths contained within this letter?

There is a Superior Person: Adore Him.
A Superior Priesthood: Approach Him.
A Superior Principle: Emulate Him.

CHAPTER 20

James

An old African American preacher once said:

"My brethren, there be two sides to the gospel. There is the believing side and there is the behaving side."

James would have agreed. We can almost hear him saying: *"Amen!"*

The book of James deals with the latter – *"the behaving side"* - for James is the most intensely practical book of the New Testament. It deals with every-day life for the man in the street.

The book is not devoid of doctrine. In this book, as Alan Cairns reminds us, we have:

- a fourfold revelation of God – James 1:17; Chapter 3:9; Chapter 4:12 and Chapter 5:4.
- a three-fold revelation of Christ – James 1:1; Chapter 2:1 and Chapter 5:9.
- a well-developed doctrine of Scripture - James 1:18-25.
- a definite doctrine of salvation – James 1:18 and Chapter 2:14-26.

However, the letter was not written for the purpose of establishing the doctrines of the faith. It is simply a practical book. This is no nonsense Christianity for daily life, where *"the rubber hits the road"*.

A student on one occasion was asked to name his favourite translation of the Bible.

Do you know what he replied?

"My mother's!"

The questioner continued: *"Is that a translation into English?"*

"No!" the student replied. *"It is a translation into action!"*

That, in a nutshell, is James' great concern.

His point is: If you say you believe, why do you act like you don't?

This book is a plea for reality- and is that not what we need today?
Many of us are long on theory but short on practice.
Many of us hear the Word but few of us heed it.
Many of us profess but few of us practise.

Notice a few things by way of introduction:

1. The Position that James Adopts

The letter begins with the name of the author: *"James"*.

Let us stop there. Three prominent men are named James in the New Testament.

There was James the son of Zebedee and brother of John.
A fisherman by trade, he was the first of the disciples to give his life for Christ. He was martyred by Herod in A.D. 44 (Acts 12:1-2).

Then there was James the son of Alphaeus. He was another one of the disciples (Matthew 10:3 and Acts 1:13).

Finally, there was James our Lord's half-brother, born and raised in the same family (Matthew 13:55; Mark 6:3 and Galatians 1:19). This James was the full brother of Jude who wrote the book of Jude. Do you recall that James was an unbeliever prior to the resurrection (John 7:5)? Then the Risen Lord appeared to him and dispelled all his former doubts (1 Corinthians 15:7). We then see him with the believers in the Upper Room (Acts 1:14). He became the key leader in the Jerusalem church (Acts 12:17; Chapter 15:13; Chapter

21:18 and Galatians 2:12) being called one of the *"pillars"* of that church, along with Peter and John.

It is generally accepted that this James wrote this book around A.D. 44-49, making it the earliest written book in the New Testament. He came to be known as: *"James, the Just"*.

Do you see how James opens this letter? *"James, a servant of God."* He did not say: *"James, the leader of the church in Jerusalem"* nor: *"James, the Lord's brother"*. Unlike some Twenty-first Century preachers who are always name-dropping, he simply says: *"James, a servant of God"*.

Someone has said:

"The great man never thinks he is great and the small man never thinks he is small."

"James, a servant of God." It means he was utterly pledged to his Master (Exodus 21:6), not only in life but also in death. You see, James came to a tragic but glorious end. In A.D. 62, the Jewish leaders captured *"James the Just"*. They took him to the pinnacle of the temple where the devil had tempted Christ (Luke 4:9). They said: *"Now blaspheme Christ or we will throw you off."* They threw him off but the fall didn't kill him and he managed to stumble to his knees to pray for his murderers. He cried: *"Father, forgive them. They do not know what they do!"* The crowd cried out: *"James the Just is praying for us"*. They finished the job by stoning him to death and James joined the roll call of the martyrs.

Tradition has it that when his fellow disciples came to pick up his body and give him a decent burial they were astonished. For the very first time they saw his knees – and they looked like the knees of a camel. Here was a man who spent more time on his knees than on his feet.

2. The Person that James Acclaims

Do you see how high James lifts his Saviour? *"James, a servant of*

God and of the Lord Jesus Christ." Do you see how James describes Him? There is a tendency in our day just to refer to Him as *"Jesus"*, but James gives Him His title and so should we: *"the Lord Jesus Christ"*. Indeed, the Master Himself said: *"Ye call me Master and Lord: and ye say well; for so I am"* (John 13:13). Was it not James' desire to uplift the Saviour?

A young preacher was once given some advice by a mature Christian of many years' experience. It was this:

"Young man, whenever you preach be sure that you do two things. Lift the Saviour high and lay the sinner low."

That is what James was doing. Is this your desire?

3. The People that James Addresses

"To the twelve tribes which are scattered abroad" (James 1:1).

"The twelve tribes" can only mean the people of Israel, the Jewish nation (Matthew 19:28; Acts 26:7 and Revelation 7:4). James sent this letter to Christian Jews. The word *"scattered"* here means: *"in the dispersion"*. It was used to mean Jews who lived outside the land of Palestine but who kept in contact with their *"fatherland"*, returning home for the feasts when possible. He is writing to Christian Jews who have been dispersed, to those who have had to leave their homes, their jobs and their properties.

Do you recall that at Stephen's death there was: *"a great persecution against the church which was at Jerusalem; and they were all scattered abroad"* (Acts 8:1)? This would have been A.D. 31-34.

Do you recall the persecution under Herod Agrippa the First? *"Now about that time Herod the king stretched forth his hands to vex certain of the church"* (Acts 12:1).

Christian Jews were scattered throughout the Roman Empire. Being Jews, they would be rejected by the Gentiles and being Christian Jews, they would be rejected by their own countrymen.

So you can see that this letter has a very Jewish emphasis. It belongs to the period before the inclusion of Gentiles into the church, when the whole church was Jewish and when their meeting places still bore the designation: *"synagogues"* (James 2:2).

4. The Problems that James Acknowledges

Basically these Jewish believers had to face two main problems.

Persecution from outside the fellowship and problems within the fellowship.

You think you have problems? Do you see what these people had to deal with?

    The problem of trials.
    The problem of temptations.
    The problem of being partial.
    The problem of worldliness.
    The problem of the tongue.
    The problem of competing as teachers within the assembly.

The matters that James deals with here are so relevant for us today.

What about:

5. The Point that James Accentuates

The point emphasised in this letter is: *"faith without works is dead"* (James 2:26).

There was a song that was popular some years ago. It was entitled: *"Love and Marriage"*. Do you remember it?

"Love and marriage, love and marriage,
Go together like a horse and carriage."

And one of the lines went like this:
"You can't have one without the other."

Faith and works go together like a horse and carriage also. *You cannot have one without the other.* Dissolve the partnership and faith dies. Faith was never designed to dwell alone, separate from the partner that proves its existence. Someone has said that faith is like calories: *"You can't see them, but you can always see their results".* That is the major theme resonating throughout James' letter - *results.*

Of course, to Martin Luther whose battle cry in the Reformation was: *"Justification by faith alone",* the battle cry of James: *"Justification by works"* was blatant heresy.

But is it really?

I think that the faith and works dispute arises when people fail to make a distinction between the *requirement for salvation* and the *result of salvation.* Good works are not the requirement but they are certainly the result.

Paul stresses the Root of salvation which is faith in Christ, plus nothing. James stresses the Fruit after salvation.

Paul sees the fire in the fireplace, but James eyes the smoke coming out of the chimney. James' whole thrust is: *"You can't have one without the other!"*

Genuine faith always produces genuine results.

If you say that you have come to know the Lord, then that should be reflected by your life.

Let us see how James develops this theme through his letter:

1. FAITH & THE CHRISTIAN'S WALK
Chapter 1

Do you recall the words of Hebrews? *"Without faith it is impossible to please Him"* (Hebrews 11:6).

Faith is the channel by which all of God's blessings come to us (Hebrews 11:6) and the reality of a man's faith always finds a definite counterpart in his life and conduct. Here in Chapter 1, faith is being tested.

James talks about:

(a) TRIALS ON THE OUTSIDE
Chapter 1 verses 1-12

The Greek word for *"temptations"* in verse 2 means: *"testings"* or *"trials"*. It indicates trouble, something that breaks the pattern of peace, comfort, joy and happiness in someone's life. It conveys the idea: *"to put someone or something to the test"*.

Remember that James is writing this letter to Jewish Christians who had been dispersed during the First Century. Rich men dragged these poor Jewish Christians before the court and blasphemed the name of the Lord Jesus by which they were called (James 2:6-7). Wealthy landowners employed them to reap their fields and then defrauded them of their rightful wages. Men had lost their jobs. Women were at their wits' end and James says: *"Count it all joy"* (James 1:2).

You might say:

"Preacher, it is hard to have joy when you are going through a trial."

I agree. Most of us would say that it is a joy when we escape trials, not a joy when we encounter trials. But, the word *"count"* here means: *"to look ahead"*. Looking ahead at what? At the end result of our trials. It is finding joy in what the trials produce. James uses the word *"perfect"* twice in verse 4:

"But let patience have her perfect work, that ye may be perfect and entire, wanting nothing."

It is a word that means: *"complete, full grown."* He is talking about spiritual maturity. The thought conveyed is that of a mature, complete Christian, *"conformed to the image of His Son"* (Romans 8:29).

Often in our trials we do not understand God's purpose.
Sometimes Satan tempts us to ask: *"Does the Lord really care?"*
This is when we need to pray for wisdom. You see, wisdom helps us to understand how to use these circumstances for our good and God's glory.

A gifted secretary of a pastor was going through great trials. She had a stroke, her husband had gone blind, and then he had been taken to hospital where he was not expected to live.
One Sunday morning in church the pastor assured her of his prayers.
But she shocked him when she said: *"Pastor, what are you asking God to do?"*
"I'm asking God to help and strengthen you", he replied.
"I appreciate that", she said. *"But pray about one thing more. Pray that I will have wisdom not to waste all of this."*

Are you in the midst of stressful trials? Do you realize that this is how God makes your faith grow? Are you praying for wisdom to discern His ways?

Then:

(b) TEMPTATIONS ON THE INSIDE
Chapter 1 verses 13-27

Having dealt with external trials, James now turns to internal temptations. Now remember there is a difference between the two.

Temptations are sent by Satan to make the Christian stumble; trials are sent by God to make the Christian stand.
In Testing you, God is aiming at your maturity.
In Tempting you, Satan is aiming at your misery.
God always tests to bring out the best, but Satan always tempts to bring out the worst.

In verse 2, James was using the word *"trial"* to mean: *"external trial"*, but here in verse 13, he is using the word *"tempted"* to mean: *"internal temptation"*.

"But every man is tempted, when he is drawn away of his own lust, and enticed. Then when lust hath conceived, it bringeth forth sin: and sin, when it is finished, bringeth forth death" (verses 14-15).

It was the late Guy King who said: *"Temptation is when you're asked to do it; sin is when you do it".*

When we think of sin, we think of it as a single act, but God sees it as a process. James describes the "birth" of sin. Enticement from without generates lust from within, lust conceives and gives birth to sin and sin brings death.

Do you see those words: *"drawn away ... enticed"*? They are taken from the world of fishing. The fisherman uses bait to lure the prey. Sometimes he will use the fly or the worm or the silver spinner on the hook. The fish are attracted by the bait. They swim towards it, open their mouths - and are on dry land before they can change their minds!

Is this not the same with us? Sin never starts with the bait, it always starts with the desire. Do you recall King David? His sin with Bathsheba came about because of his internal desire to play outside the boundaries of God. David was out of God's will. He was in the palace when, as the Bible says, it was *"the time when kings go forth to battle"* (2 Samuel 11:1). So what happened? Satan baited the hook with an external force. Her name was Bathsheba. David took the bait.

Is Satan dangling a bait in front of you? What is her name, his name, its name? Are you allowing your desires to get out of line with God's desires? Do you know what will sustain you in the hour of trial and strengthen you in the moment of temptation? The Word of God.

Here James tells us that as God's people, we should:

Hear the Word – verses 19-20
Receive the Word – verse 21, and
Obey the Word – verse 22.
We could write over this section: ***"The Christian and his Bible"***.

Do you want to walk with the Lord? Well, how much time do you spend in your Bible?

John Bunyan said: *"I was never out of my Bible"*.
John Wesley said: *"I am a man of one book"*.

Are you? Can you say: *"O how I love Thy law! it is my meditation all the day"* (Psalm 119:97)?

(2) FAITH & THE CHRISTIAN'S WORSHIP
Chapter 2

In verse 2 of Chapter 2, the Greek word translated *"assembly"* is the word for *"synagogue"*, showing us again how Jewish this letter is.

James here is talking about worship. He is speaking about:

(a) FAITH AND LOVE
Chapter 2 verses 1-13

James is saying that faith is proved by love.

Look at verse 1:

"My brethren, have not the faith of our Lord Jesus Christ, the Lord of glory, with respect of persons."

The Amplified Bible puts it like this: *"Do not attempt to hold and practise the faith of our Lord Jesus Christ, the Lord of glory, together with snobbery."*

It raises its head then and it raises its head now. Someone has said there are at least five areas where we as believers can be tempted to discriminate.

We can discriminate on the basis of appearance, ancestry, age, achievement and affluence.

Let us try and get the picture here. Imagine you are the usher at a worship service and in walk two men. *Mr. Have followed by Mr. Have-Not.* The first is wearing a £500 suit. He has been to some fancy shop in the town. The other man comes in wearing clothes from a charity shop. You are enamoured with outward appearance and so you escort the rich man to the best seat. You say to the poor man: *"Go and stand over there, out of the way!"* The real problem is not finding a good seat for the rich man but in ignoring the poor man.

Are we guilty of this sort of thing? Do you look down your nose at some other believers because you think you are better off than they are? Are you indifferent to some because of their poor position? Because of their unattractive outward appearance? If so, we are guilty of breaking *"the royal law"* (James 2:8): *"Thou shalt love thy neighbour as thyself"* (Leviticus 19:18, 34; Matthew 22:34-40 and Galatians 5:14).

Do you know something? We need to see everyone through the eyes of Christ. Is that how you look on others? By accepting them for what they are and seeing them as individuals for whom Christ died?

(b) FAITH AND WORKS
Chapter 2 verses 14-26

James is saying that faith is proved by works.

As already mentioned, this section of James has caused some undue concern among Christians. Does James contradict Paul on the question of justification by faith alone?

Well, it would be hard for him to do this! At the time James wrote - A.D. 44-49 - Paul had yet to finish the first line of his many letters.

But there is no contradiction.

In the book of Romans, Paul is explaining how the sinner is justified, given a right standing before God.
In the book of James, James is explaining how the saved person proves that salvation before others.

You see, a sinner is saved by faith without works, but true saving faith leads to works.

James names two Old Testament people to prove his point: Abraham and Rahab. Let us take the first one, Abraham. Look at verse 21:

"Was not Abraham our father justified by works, when he had offered Isaac his son upon the altar?"

The question is: When was Abraham justified?

Think about:

The Moment of Abraham's Justification

When was he justified? Well, look at verse 23:

"And the scripture was fulfilled which saith, Abraham believed God, and it was imputed unto him for righteousness: and he was called the Friend of God."

This is a quote from Genesis 15 verse 6. You see, Abraham's salvation experience is recorded in Genesis 15, thirty years before this incident on Mount Moriah, thirty years before he offered up Isaac.

God came to Abraham and told him he would have a son and that his seed would be as the stars in the heaven. Do you recall Abraham's response? *"And he believed in the LORD; and He counted*

125

it to him for righteousness" (Genesis 15:16). Paul says exactly the same thing in Romans 4 verse 3: *"Abraham believed God, and it was counted unto him for righteousness"*. He was justified by faith. Justification is that act of God in which He declares righteous the sinner who believes on Christ. It is not a process - it is an act. It is not something the sinner does - it is something God does for the sinner when he trusts Christ.

So, this was the moment of Abraham's justification. But notice:

The Mark of Abraham's Justification

People who say that James contradicts Paul say that because they fail to see that James was not referring here to Genesis 15, the moment Abraham exercised faith in God, but rather to Genesis 22, the moment Abraham offered up Isaac.

You see, the offering up of Isaac was not the moment of Abraham's justification, but it was the mark of Abraham's justification.

The Amplified Bible puts it like this: *"Was not Abraham our father shown to be justified by his works?"*

In the words of Matthew Poole:

"Abraham's justification was not the absolution of a sinner but the approbation of a saint."

The offering up of Isaac was the proof, the evidence, the sign that the faith he had exercised in Genesis 15 was real, saving faith. A faith that does not produce works is dead and useless.

Do you see the closing words of verse 14? It ought to read: *"Can that kind of faith save him?"*

It was John Calvin who said: ***"Faith alone saves but the faith that saves is not alone!"***

What a word for our land! This country is filled with people who have signed a card, raised a hand, joined a church, made a profession, but let us face the challenge of God's Word.

"Show me thy faith" (verse 18). Will your faith get you to Heaven? Is it a faith that works?

(3) FAITH & THE CHRISTIAN'S WORDS
Chapter 3

You get the impression when you read this letter that the believers to whom James wrote were having serious problems with their tongues. Five times over in this short letter, James brings this subject up: James 1:19, 26; Chapter 2:12; Chapter 4:11 and Chapter 5:12. It seems evident that what Matthew Henry calls *"the sins of the tongue"* were rather prevalent among these Christians. Would James find them less common if he were to visit our churches today?

The Tongue! Medically, they say it is only a two or three inch slab of muscle, mucous membrane and nerves that enable us to chew, taste and swallow. It is also the major organ of communication that enables us to articulate distinct sounds so that we can understand each other. How vital this strange muscle in our mouth! But how volatile as well!

It was Washington Irving who said:

"A sharp tongue is the only edge tool that grows keener with constant use."

It was James who said: *"the tongue is a fire, a world of iniquity"* (James 3:6). No wonder he begins this chapter with:

(a) THE EXHORTATION
Chapter 3 verses 1-2

The Chapter opens:

"My brethren, be not many masters."

The word *"masters"* is teachers. Now, James is not condemning the teaching ministry, but he is warning against clamouring for the position without carefully weighing the cost. You see, those of us who teach the Word of God will be judged more strictly than most. Great privileges bring great responsibilities (Luke 12:48). The writer to the Hebrews reminds us that elders are to be obeyed. Why? *"For they watch for your souls, as they that must give account"* (Hebrews 13:17). Of course, all of us stumble in many ways, especially in what we say.

James sets before us here:

(b) THE EXPLANATION
Chapter 3 verses 3-12

He explains to us how the tongue works. He tells us that the tongue has:

Power to Direct: the Bit and Rudder (verses 3-4)

The word *"helm"* in verse 4 is: *"rudder"*. A horse is controlled by reins and a ship is controlled by a rudder. There are young folk who do not know the way to go, but a *"bit"* of word from you and me could set the direction of their lives for God and good.

As a young man, I conducted a week's mission. At the conclusion of the week, an older brother said to me: *"Denis, take the next step"* – and that word changed the whole direction of my life.

I think of the older generation, so many of them battling across life's ocean, often *"driven of fierce winds"*, sometimes not knowing where to find a haven of peace.

Are such people near you? Are you willing to be a Barnabas to them?

Power to Destroy: The Fire and the Animal (verses 5-8)

Do you know that your words can start fires?

Proverbs 26 verses 20 to 22 put it like this:

"Where no wood is, there the fire goeth out: so where there is no talebearer, the strife ceaseth. As coals are to burning coals, and wood to fire; so is a contentious man to kindle strife. The words of a talebearer are as wounds, and they go down into the innermost parts of the belly."

Did you know your tongue is like a wild beast that cannot be tamed?

Power to Delight: The Fountain and the Tree (verses 9-12)

It is impossible for a fountain to produce both fresh water and salt. Likewise a tree cannot bear two kinds of fruit. Yet, how often we speak with forked tongues.

Do you see how inconsistent we are?

James concludes this chapter with:

(c) THE EXPRESSION
   Chapter 3 verses 13-18

James compares the critical tongue and the controlled tongue by the wisdom they express.

The critical tongue is worldly-wise in its expression, while the controlled tongue is heavenly-wise in its expression.

An Egyptian king named Amasis once sent a sacrifice to his god and asked the priest to send back the best and worst parts of the animal. The priest sent back the tongue, which organ said he represented both demands.

(4) FAITH & THE CHRISTIAN'S WARFARE
Chapter 4

Franklin D. Roosevelt once said: *"There is nothing I love so much as a good fight!"*

Fighting is something that comes to us naturally. Why? Because we are each born with a scrappy nature that prefers going for the jugular than giving in. Now it is evident that these Christians were fighting and squabbling among themselves.

James speaks here of:

(a) THE SPIRITUAL WAR
Chapter 4 verses 1-12

There was *War on a Relational Level.*
The Amplified Bible puts verse 1 like this: *"What leads to strife and how do conflicts originate among you?"* Among whom? Among Christians!

There was *Social Rivalry:*	between rich and poor (James 2:1).
There was *Ecclesiastical Jealousy:*	between the teachers and the taught (James 3:1).
There was *Personal Enmity:*	(James 4:11) It seems these Christians were speaking evil of one another.

There was War on an Internal Level: Look at verse 1 again. The war in the heart was helping to cause the wars in the church. We are at war with each other, because we are at war with ourselves. Do you see the root of the problem? *"Your lusts"* - *"Your desires"* or *"Your selfish satisfaction"* (verse 1). Is this not the essence of sin? Selfishness. People wanting to get their own way in marriage, in work, in school, in the assembly.

There was War on a Vertical Level: How does a Christian declare war on God? By being friendly with God's enemies. And they are all here! In verse 1, you have got the flesh; in verse 4, you have got the world, and in verse 7, you have got the devil. If you live for the world and the flesh you will become proud and the devil will take advantage of you. Pride is one of his chief tools.

How can we overcome? With:

(b) THE SUBMISSIVE WILL
Chapter 4 verses 13-17

We need to Acknowledge the Priority of God

Back in verse 7, James has declared: *"Submit yourselves therefore to God"*. It was a military term, speaking of someone getting into his proper rank.
Have you put yourself under the Lordship of Christ?

We need to Acknowledge the Presence of God

Back in verse 8, James has declared: *"Draw nigh to God"*. If we are going to be victorious in the battle, we need to utilise all the resources that God puts at our disposal.

We need to Acknowledge the Prerogative of God

We need to stamp: **"D.V."** (God willing!) over all our plans, hopes and aspirations.

Do you do that? Do you bring the Lord into your plans? Is He Lord in every area of your life?

(5) FAITH & AND THE CHRISTIAN'S WAITING
Chapter 5

The key thought in this last chapter seems to be the Second Coming of Christ and how we are to live in the light of it.

"Be patient therefore, brethren, unto the coming of the Lord. Behold, the husbandman waiteth for the precious fruit of the earth, and hath long patience for it, until he receive the early and latter rain. Be ye also patient; stablish your hearts: for the coming of the Lord draweth nigh" (verses 7-8).

James says:

(a) BE HOPEFUL
Chapter 5 verses 1-11

James mentions the sins of the rich: hoarding (verses 1-3), stealing (verse 4) and killing (verse 6). James encourages these believers to get their eyes on the coming of the Lord (verse 7). James was saying: *"Do not let momentary stumbles beset you. Look up and be calm!"*

"Be patient ... unto the coming of the Lord."
Is the coming of Christ not both comforting and challenging?
Comforting because we shall see Christ.
Challenging because He will search us at the Judgment Seat (verse 9).

What a solemn moment that will be! It will not matter how far up the social ladder we have climbed or what car we drove or what kind of house we lived in. The only thing that will count in that day will be our service for the Lord.

(b) BE TRUTHFUL
Chapter 5 verse 12

James is not forbidding the taking of oaths in a court of law. In Matthew 26 verse 63, the Lord Jesus was put on oath. James is simply saying that the Christian must always keep his word.

(c) BE PRAYERFUL
Chapter 5 verses 13-18

Prayer is to be corporate (verse 14), dependent (verse 15), powerful (verse 16) and exemplary (verse 17).

Elijah was remembered for the power of his prayer life. Will we be?
James was remembered for the regularity of his prayer life. Again, will we be?

(d) BE FAITHFUL
Chapter 5 verses 19-20

"Brethren, if any of you do err from the truth, and one convert him; Let him know, that he which converteth the sinner from the error of his way, shall save a soul from death, and shall hide a multitude of sins" (verses 19-20)

It is so easy to be wrapped up in our trials that we forget the needs of the lost and of Christians who have strayed.

The word *"err"* means: *"to wander"*. Like the sheep of Matthew 18 verse 12 that *"is gone astray"*.

Is that us? Do we need to sing?

> *"Prone to wander, Lord, I feel it,*
> *Prone to leave the God I love."*

Have you wandered away from the Lord? Do you know someone who has? They once sat with us at the Lord's Supper, they once stood with us in the Open Air, they once knelt with us at the throne of grace, but where are they today?

Do you see that word: *"convert"*? It means: *"to turn back"*.

Do you know something? That is *our* responsibility. The word *"one"* means: *"someone"*. It is the responsibility of the person in the pulpit and also the responsibility of the person in the pew. James is saying that we have been given the ministry of restoration. Now that is the basic interpretation, but we can apply it to the lost. After all, if an erring brother needs to be restored, how much more does a lost sinner to be saved?

The sandglass of prophecy is running out. *"The coming of the Lord draweth nigh."* But what about our unsaved family? Do we need to pray afresh?

> *"Oh, give us all a passion,*
> *For souls as ne'er before,*
> *To warn men and to tell them,*
> *The Judge is at the door."*

CHAPTER 21

1 Peter

David Pawson, in writing about 1 Peter, reminds us of the Great Fire of London which started on 2ⁿᵈ September 1666. It began in a baker's shop in Pudding Lane and caused tremendous damage. Most of the houses were timber-framed and so were unable to withstand the flames. One-third of the city was destroyed and over one hundred thousand people lost their homes. The damage caused was estimated at £10,000,000. About 90 churches were destroyed, although many of them were later rebuilt by Sir Christopher Wren, including St. Paul's Cathedral.

Of course, when there is a disaster, human nature tends to look around for a scapegoat, for someone to blame. In the case of the Great Fire of London, the finger was pointed at the French Catholics.

Now, as we come to this letter of 1 Peter, I want you to think about:

1. THE ATMOSPHERE OF THIS LETTER

The fire in London took place in 1666, but on 19ᵗʰ July 64 A.D. a fire began in the city of Rome. It lasted three days, devastating much of the city. It engulfed the centre of Rome, destroying temples and houses. The citizens of Rome knew that Nero had ambitions to pull down old buildings and to erect new magnificent structures. They, therefore, assumed that he was behind it. Nero, however, managed to divert suspicion from himself to the Christians.

The result? A savage outbreak of persecution! The believers faced awful times. The persecution started about November of 64 A.D.

and lasted under Nero's death in 68 A.D. It was not just confined to Rome but it spread more or less throughout the whole Empire. Christians were tortured. Nero rolled them in pitch and then set light to them while they were still alive. He used them as living torches to light his gardens. He sewed them in skins of wild animals and then set wild dogs upon them to tear them limb from limb. Christians were tied to chariots and dragged through the streets of Rome until dead. They were thrown to the lions. They were sealed up in leather bags and thrown into the water so that when the leather bags shrank, they were squeezed and suffocated to death.

This was the backcloth against which Peter wrote this letter. Indeed there are clues here that tell us that persecution was raging when this letter was penned somewhere between 64-65 A.D.

"That the trial of your faith, being much more precious than of gold that perisheth, though it be tried with fire, might be found unto praise and honour and glory at the appearing of Jesus Christ" (1 Peter 1:7).

"Beloved, think it not strange concerning the fiery trial which is to try you, as though some strange thing happened unto you" (1 Peter 4:12).

The atmosphere of the letter: Nero's persecutions – and this letter needs to be read in the light of that background.

2. THE AUTHOR OF THIS LETTER

The letter commences: *"Peter, an apostle of Jesus Christ"*.

Here he gives us **His name**: *"Peter"*; **His vocation**: *"an apostle"*, and **His Lord**: *"Jesus Christ"*. He had been sent by Christ to speak of Christ (John 21:15). This letter is also associated with Silvanus or Silas (1 Peter 5:12). He was one of the *"chief men"* in the early church (Acts 15:22) and a prophet (Acts 15:32).

Peter does *not* begin: *"Peter, the bishop of the church at Rome"*.

Nor does he begin: *"Peter, the chief shepherd"*. In Chapter 5 verse

4, he gives that title – *"Chief Shepherd"* – to the Lord Jesus, while modestly describing himself in verse 1 of that Chapter as: *"an elder"*.

No, Peter begins: *"Peter, an apostle of Jesus Christ"*.

Peter is not writing as the Vicar of Christ, the Pope of Rome. He knows no such title, no such position. He has a greater position, one he shared with the rest of the apostles, but it was a disappearing office. The work of the apostle was to lay the foundation of the church (Ephesians 2:20). With the death of a dozen men, this unique position would vanish forever from the earth. While it lasted, it gave Peter a status not given to many but shared equally with others.

Peter was an apostle, one of a small group of men to whom the Lord Jesus entrusted the spread of the gospel. These *"sent ones"* could have, in the strictest sense of the term, no successors.

"Peter, an apostle of Jesus Christ" - restored and reinstated and recommissioned by his Master.

Do you recall the Saviour's words to him? *"When thou art converted (turned back, restored), strengthen thy brethren"* (Luke 22:32). Later, the risen Christ said to Peter: *"Feed My sheep"* (John 21:16).

Do you know something? The writing of this letter was part of that ministry.

A lot of controversy surrounds **the place** where Peter wrote this letter. Look at Chapter 5 verses 12 and 13:

"By Silvanus, a faithful brother unto you, as I suppose, I have written briefly, exhorting, and testifying that this is the true grace of God wherein ye stand. The church that is at Babylon, elected together with you, saluteth you; and so doth Marcus my son."

Now there are two main theories concerning this location.

One is *literal Babylon* on the Euphrates River - and this would seem to be the natural interpretation.

Other Bible scholars feel that *"Babylon"* is an pseudonym for Rome, perhaps even a code word for Rome. Dr. Charles Ryrie writes: *"The place of the writing was Babylon, a symbolic name for Rome, much used by writers who wished to avoid trouble with Roman authorities".* You see, in times of persecution, writers would exercise unusual care not to endanger Christians by identifying them.

Wherever we believe that Peter wrote this letter from, whether literal Babylon or *symbolic Babylon*, one thing is sure. These believers had their backs against the wall.

Consider for a moment:

3. THE AUDIENCE OF THIS LETTER

Do you see how verse 1 concludes?

"to the strangers scattered throughout Pontus, Galatia, Cappadocia, Asia, and Bithynia."

These believers lived in a far-flung region of the Roman Empire covering the area now belonging to Turkey. There were Jews at Pentecost from Pontus and Cappadocia (Acts 2:9) so perhaps they had returned home with the message of Christ. Moreover, Paul had founded churches in Asia Minor (Acts 18:23). People were *"on the move"* in those days and dedicated believers shared the Word wherever they went (Acts 8:4).

Now, do you notice how Peter describes these believers? He says they were:

(a) A Strange People

"Strangers." The word means: *"resident aliens, sojourners."* In Chapter 2 verse 11, Peter refers to them as: *"strangers and pilgrims".* Most of the people to whom Peter was writing were Jewish

converts (1 Peter 2:12 and Chapter 3:6), but Gentile believers were also in the mind of the apostle (1 Peter 1:14 and Chapter 4:3). In both cases, however, the temporariness of their abode is implied by the word *"sojourner"*. Do you recall what Paul says? *"Our citizenship is in heaven"* (Philippians 3:20). We are a little colony of Heaven on earth. Do we not sing it?

> *"This world is not my home,*
> *I'm just a passing through,*
> *My treasures are laid up,*
> *Somewhere beyond the blue."*

The problem with many of us today is that where they spoke of passing through we talk about settling down!

Are you cultivating the spirit of the pilgrim and stranger? Or have you got your roots so far down in the world's soil that the temporal have crowded out the spiritual, the material has crowded out the eternal, the things of this earth has crowded out the things of God?

Peter says they were a strange people. He also says they were:

(b) A Scattered People

"To the strangers scattered." *"Scattered"* literally means: *"Dispersion"*. This was a technical term for the Jews who lived outside of Israel (John 7:35). Here, however, it applied to believers, Jewish and Gentiles, who were scattered in five different parts of the Roman Empire. Scholars tell us that the origin of the word *"dispersion"* can be traced to the Greek words: *"dia speiro"*. The word *"dia"* means: *"throughout"* and the word *"speiro"* means: *"to sow seed"*. So it literally means: *"scattered seed"*.

We are scattered as seed throughout the world so that we may sow seed in the world.

Seed left in the barn is absolutely useless and ultimately will rot, but if it is scattered throughout the fields, it will bear fruit.

Is it not amazing where God in His providence places us? Beside that needy neighbour, in that godless office, on that factory floor, in that hospital ward. Providentially placed by God to sow the seed of the Word of God.

We are not aliens in the world, but we are to be ambassadors to the world.

> "I am a stranger here,
> Within a foreign land,
> My home is far away,
> Upon a golden strand;
> Ambassador to be,
> Of realms beyond the sea,
> I'm here on business
> For my King."

Why did Peter write this letter?

4. THE AIM OF THIS LETTER

Remember again the background. Nero is doing terrible things to the Christians. They were up against it and so Peter writes to encourage them.

He says in verse 12 of Chapter 5:

"By Silvanus, a faithful brother unto you, as I suppose, I have written briefly, exhorting, and testifying that this is the true grace of God wherein ye stand."

That word *"exhorted"* can be translated: *"encouraging"*. Peter is encouraging them to stand fast in the true grace of God.

Did you know that the word *"grace"* is used almost in every chapter of Peter? 1 Peter 1 verses 2, 10 and 13; Chapter 3 verse 7; Chapter 4 verse 10 and Chapter 5 verses 5, 10 and 12.

Moreover, in the final chapter Peter speaks about: *"the God of all grace"* (1 Peter 5:10).

What is grace? It is the unmerited favour of God to undeserving sinners and needy saints. It is God's provision for our need when we need it. The believer is to go from grace to grace (John 1:16). James says: *"He giveth more grace"* (James 4:6). It is *grace* alone that *saves* us (Ephesians 2:8-10), but God's *grace* can also *sustain* us in the trials of life.

Are you like these believers? Are you facing trials, hardships and difficulties? Well, look at this letter and let it bring encouragement to your soul.

(1) THE CHRISTIAN'S SALVATION
Chapter 1 verse 1 to Chapter 2 verse 10

Peter is saying to these suffering saints:

"I want to remind you of what a wonderful salvation we have, a salvation that triumphs over even the terror of the grave."

So what does Peter do? He picks up three of Paul's favourite words: faith, hope and love and, as John Phillips says: *"weaves them into a glorious garland of encouragement"*.

Paul is the apostle of faith, John is the apostle of love and Peter is the apostle of hope. Faith that looks back to the past; hope that looks forward to the future, and love that deals with the present. Past, present and future are all embraced in God's *"so great salvation"*.

In these opening verses we see:

(a) The Doctrine of Salvation Expounded
Chapter 1 verses 1-5

Peter relates the Doctrine of Salvation to our Past

These believers were being persecuted, pressurised and criticised. They may have been *"nobodies"* in the eyes of the world, but they were *"special"* in the eyes of God, for *the Father Elected them, the*

Spirit Separated them, and the Son Cleansed them. They were the objects of God's electing, everlasting love.

Now, election is a mystery in our comprehension, but a blessing in our apprehension.

Election is one of those family truths that are taught in the Bible that we cannot understand fully. Yet, because God teaches it, we accept it and we are blessed because of it.

Does this not warm your heart and uplift your spirit?

You were in God's plan from all eternity. Then God the Spirit set you apart to Himself, and the blood of Christ cleansed you. Is it not great to be saved?

This salvation is the work of the Triune God bringing us to salvation.

> *The Plan: The Father Thought it.*
> *The Power: The Spirit Brought it.*
> *The Price: The Son Bought it.*

As far as God the Father is concerned, I was saved when He chose me in Christ before the foundation of the world.

As far as the Son is concerned, I was saved when He died for me on the Cross.

As far as the Holy Spirit is concerned, I was saved when as a lad of 9 years of age I knelt at my father's knee and received Christ as my Saviour.

What do we have now? New life! The word *"begotten"* in verse 3: *"begotten us again unto a lively hope"* reminds us of Christ's statement to Nicodemus in verse 7 of John 3: *"Ye must be born again"*.

Peter relates the Doctrine of Salvation to our Present

Peter says we are: *"kept by the power of God"* (verse 5). That word *"kept"* is a military word. It means: *"guarded, shielded"*. It would have been used in the context of keeping prisoners in a castle. There was absolutely no chance of them escaping.

Do not ever get the idea that you keep yourself saved. We are kept by the power of God.

Peter relates the Doctrine of Salvation to our Future

Peter says we have: *"a living hope"* (verse 3).

This hope is grounded on the living Word of God (1 Peter 1:23) and is made possible by the living Son of God who triumphed over death. Because of Christ's resurrection, we are absolutely sure of future glory and blessing. Peter describes this glory as: *"an inheritance"* (verse 4). An inheritance is something you get. It is something that is yours out there in the future. Do you see how Peter describes it? *Undying; Undefiled; Unfading and Unfailing.*

Do you ever pause to count your blessings? Do you lift up your heart in praise to God for such a hope?

(b) The Doctrine of Salvation Experienced
Chapter 1 verses 6-9

In these verses, Peter talks about the trials of salvation. Do you recall the context? Peter is writing to Christians who were in the throes of a violent persecution that robbed them of all their earthly comforts. Their faith was being tested, but then **the faith that cannot be tested cannot be trusted.**

"That the trial of your faith, being much more precious than of gold that perisheth, though it be tried with fire, might be found unto praise and honour and glory at the appearing of Jesus Christ" (verse 7).

That word *"trial"* conveys the picture of a precious metal being heated until it is liquid. Its impurities then rise to the top and are scraped off. Only pure metal is left.

Is this not the purpose of our trials? To purge us of impurity? To burn out the dross and to leave us cleansed and purified?

There is a dependable wisdom that chooses every thread in the pattern, so that we may confidently say:

> "The dark threads are as needful,
> In the Weaver's skilful hand,
> As the threads of gold and silver,
> In the pattern He has planned."

Now Peter is still writing about this wonderful salvation and, in verses 10 to 12, he reminds us that the Old Testament prophets spoke of the salvation we enjoy.

(c) The Doctrine of Salvation Explored
Chapter 1 verses 10-12

The prophets explored it, but often did not understand what they had written (Matthew 13:17). They could not unravel words from God that spoke of a *Sovereign Christ* and a *Suffering Christ*. They knew that they had written Scripture, but they could not grasp its significance. But, says Peter, the Holy Spirit has made it clear to us.

The sufferings of Christ were to come first, the glory was to follow.
First, the Cross, then the crown.
Christ came first to redeem, He is coming back to reign.
The literal fulfilment of the one is the guarantee of the literal fulfilment of the other.

Then Peter adds something of great interest: *"Which things the angels desire to look into"* (verse 12). Is this not amazing? That the angels are absorbed with the suffering/glory story of Christ? Why! if the angels find ever fresh fields of interest in the sufferings of Christ and the glory that should follow, should not we also?

The doctrine of salvation is expounded and experienced and explored – and then:

(d) The Doctrine of Salvation Exhibited
Chapter 1 verse 13 to Chapter 2 verse 10

In other words, how does salvation manifest itself in our lives?

Well, there will be *a Holiness like the Lord.* (1 Peter 1:13-21)

What do you think when you hear the word: *"holy"*?

Do you think of someone who has been *"stewed in vinegar"*? Sour? Always speaking a super-religious language?

Well, actually this word *"holy"* means: *"different, set apart."*

Holy people are set apart in that their lives are different from the world and are dedicated to God.

Do you know what would motivate you to be holy?

You would be motivated to be holy if you thought of the *Lord's Return* (verse 13); the *Lord's Character* (verses 15-16); the *Lord's Judgment* (verse 17) and the *Lord's Death* (verse 18).

Do you recall the prayer of Robert Murray McCheyne?

"Lord, make me as holy as it is possible for a saved sinner to be."

How does salvation manifest itself?

There will be *a Harmony in the Church.* (1 Peter 1:22 to Chapter 2:10)

We are children in the same family (1 Peter 2:1-3).
We are stones in the same building (1 Peter 2:4-8).
We are priests in the same temple (1 Peter 2:9-10).

Should that not motivate us to *"love one another"* (1 Peter 1:22)?

How does salvation manifest itself?

There will be *a Hunger for the Word.* (1 Peter 1:22 to Chapter 2:3)

"As newborn babes, desire the sincere milk of the word, that ye may grow thereby" (1 Peter 2:2).

Do you see that word *"desire"?* It means: *"to long for".* It is the picture of an earnest intense desire for the Word of God.

Do you want to know if you are saved?

Do you want to know if your sins are forgiven?

Do you want to know if you are Heaven bound?

Well, have you got an appetite for the Word?

(2) THE CHRISTIAN'S SUBMISSION
Chapter 2 verse 11 to Chapter 3 verse 12

You see, though these First Century Christians lived under persecution, they still had certain obligations. Here Peter talks about our responsibilities:

(a) CIVILLY
Chapter 2 verses 11-17

Our responsibilities as citizens.

"Submit yourselves to every ordinance of man for the Lord's sake" (verse 13).

The word *"ordinance"* means: *"creation or institution".* It does not refer to each individual law, but to the institutions that make and enforce the law. Is it not important that we respect the office even though we cannot respect the man or women in the office? God does not promote anarchy. The Lord Jesus Christ said: *"Render therefore unto Caesar the things which are Caesar's; and unto God the things that are God's"* (Matthew 22:21).

In verse 17, Peter gives an instruction: *"Honour the King".* But the King here is Nero! He is the one dragging Christians to their death behind his chariot and using them as living torches in his garden. Honour him? Surely Peter must be out of his mind! Yet that is God's Word to us. We are not told to fight, to demonstrate, to organize protest rallies and marches. We are told to submit. Do you see the motive? *"For the Lord's sake."* We obey because we want to honour the Lord and imitate the Lord Jesus *"who, when He was reviled, reviled not again; when He suffered, He threatened not; but committed Himself to Him that judgeth righteously"* (verse 23).

Are you an example in civil obedience? When it comes to filling in the tax forms, to driving the car, to keeping the law, are we model citizens?

(b) SOCIALLY
Chapter 2 verses 18-25

Peter is taking us to the workplace and telling slaves to be submissive to their masters. Look how the section commences in verse 18:

"Servants, be subject to your masters with all fear; not only to the good and gentle, but also to the froward."

The word *"froward"* means: *"crooked, perverse, dishonest"*. Those who are unreasonable.

Do you have an uncaring boss?

Do you have a supervisor or a manager who is not fair?

Do you have to deal with unreasonable people?

Do you feel like fighting back against unfair treatment? Don't! Anyone can hit back, but it takes a Spirit-filled Christian to submit and let God fight His battle.

No-one was ever more *"ripped off"* than Christ. He was the only perfect man who ever lived yet He was misunderstood, maligned, hated, arrested, tortured and crucified.

Peter says we are to walk in His steps.

Now, it is important that we distinguish here between the expiatory nature of Christ's sufferings and the exemplary nature of His sufferings.

His **expiatory suffering** as the one sacrifice for sin finds no parallel in our sufferings.
But the **exemplary nature** of Christ's suffering is set before us that we should: *"follow His steps".*

He suffering *Sinlessly* (verse 22); *Silently* (verse 23) and *Submissively* (verse 23).

He has left us an example. Are we following His steps?

(c) DOMESTICALLY
Chapter 3 verses 1-7

The trouble with most marriages today is that people are standing up for their rights, but this passage has all to do with responsibilities.

What is the responsibility of a wife? *Submission, even to unconverted husbands.* When a wife gets saved before a husband, she thinks that the one thing she must do is preach at him.

Peter says: *"Stop nagging at him and live Christ before him".*

Such a lifestyle has been called: *"the silent preaching of a lovely life".*

Does your spouse see that in you?

Conversely, husbands are to be considerate. Peter says: *"dwell with them according to knowledge"* (verse 7). Get to know your wife. Find out what makes her tick.

How are we getting on in the home?

Then there is to be submission:

(d) *CORPORATELY*
Chapter 3 verses 8-12

Look at verses 8 and 9:

"Finally, be ye all of one mind, having compassion one of another, love as brethren, be pitiful, be courteous: Not rendering evil for evil, or railing for railing: but contrariwise blessing; knowing that ye are thereunto called, that ye should inherit a blessing."

To return evil for good is unnatural.
To return evil for evil is natural.
To return good for evil is supernatural!

We are to cultivate Christian love.

Vance Havner once said:

"The Christian ought to develop a hide as tough as a rhino and a heart as tender as a baby, but the trick is how to toughen the one without toughening the other."

It takes a Christ-like spirit to submit ourselves to those who are over us, whether that it is in the workplace, the home, in society or in the church, but the great incentive to such a life is the knowledge of the Omniscience of God, *for His eyes see us, His ears hear us and His face cheers us.*

"For the eyes of the Lord are over the righteous, and His ears are open unto their prayers: but the face of the Lord is against them that do evil" (verse 12).

(3) THE CHRISTIAN'S SUFFERING
Chapter 3 verse 14 to Chapter 4 verse 19

In the midst of Peter's teaching on suffering, he makes a statement that is difficult to understand:

"For Christ also hath once suffered for sins, the just for the unjust, that He might bring us to God, being put to death in the flesh, but quickened by the Spirit: By which also He went and preached unto the spirits in prison; Which sometime were disobedient, when once the longsuffering of God waited in the days of Noah, while the ark was a preparing, wherein few, that is, eight souls were saved by water" (1 Peter 3:18-20).

Now scholars tell us that the end of verse 18 should read like this:

"being put to death with reference to the flesh but made alive with reference to the spirit."

Let me quote Robert Gundry:

"This probably means that, during the time between His death and resurrection, Christ descended in spirit form into hell (2 Peter 2:4 "tartarus"; Jude 6 and Genesis 6:1) to proclaim His triumph over the demonic spirits whom God had imprisoned there because of their corruptive influence among men in the time immediately prior to the flood."

You may agree or disagree with this statement, but the point of the passage is this:

Just as God had vindicated Christ before the very spirits who had tried to thwart God's purpose in history, so also the Lord will someday vindicate Christians before their persecutors.

Although the United Kingdom is generally free of persecution, we can anticipate increasing pressure. There has been the liberalization of marriage laws and churches will face pressure to change their stance on homosexuality.

Can you foresee a day when preachers will be put in prison because they refused to marry those of the same sex?
Can you see a time when God's servants will be harassed because they criticized another faith? In fact, it has already happened in our land.

"Suffering for righteousness" (1 Peter 3:14) could increase in our land.

Peter tells us that suffering does three things:

(a) Suffering Purifies the Believer
Chapter 3 verse 13 to Chapter 4 verse 6

When life is easy, we drift into carelessness and sin, but suffering changes our values and goals.

Suffering identifies us with Christ (1 Peter 4:1). Christ suffered for us that He might save us from sin. As we suffer for Him and with Him, we learn to hate sin and love Christ more.

Suffering changes our perspective. We take life for granted until we have to suffer, and then our values change.

Suffering points ahead to a coming judgment. You know, we all live by the judgment of men or by the judgment of God. *Have you discovered that your close friends have changed now that you are in Christ?* Are they judging you? Criticising you? Mocking you?

God is going to judge them unless they too repent and get saved.

It is better to suffer for Christ and go to be with Him than to follow the world and go to hell.

(b) Suffering Unifies the Church
Chapter 4 verses 7-11

Peter reminds them that Jesus Christ is coming soon and that in the midst of their suffering the believers have responsibilities to one another.

They are to *live consistently* (verse 7).
They are to *love continually* (verses 8-9).
They are to *labour conscientiously* (verses 10-11).

The great preacher F.B. Meyer once asked D.L. Moody: *"What is the secret of your success?"* Moody replied: *"For many years I have never given an address without the consciousness that the Lord may come before I have finished."*

Does that explain the intensity of Moody's service or the zeal of his ministry for Christ?

(c) Suffering Glorifies the Lord
Chapter 4 verses 12-19

Make sure that you do not deserve your suffering. If you go to prison for a crime, then you certainly cannot say that you are suffering for Christ. There is a suffering that is **deserved** that comes into the life of a believer.

"But let none of you suffer as a murderer, or as a thief, or as an evildoer, or as a busybody in other men's matters" (verse 15).

There are lots of Christians who are busybodies. They are always sticking their noses in someone else's business. *They go around prying when they should be praying.* Then someone fires back at them and they say: *"Oh, I am suffering for Jesus!"* No, you are not! You are just a meddler! Mind your own business!

There is a suffering that is deserved, but there is a suffering that is **derived**, that is, it comes because we are Christ's - we should seek to glorify Him.

"Yet if any man suffer as a Christian, let him not be ashamed; but let him glorify God on this behalf" (verse 16).

"Not be ashamed" – that is the negative.
"Glorify God" – that is the positive.

Do you see Peter how finishes this section?

"Wherefore let them that suffer according to the will of God commit the keeping of their souls to Him in well doing, as unto a faithful Creator" (verse 19).

Peter is saying: *Trust the faithful God.*

In the midst of your *"fiery trial"* say:

"Lord, I do not know what You are doing and I do not know the purpose of all this in my life, but, Lord, I place my life in Your care."

God is faithful and He will hold you, sustain you and keep you.

(4) THE CHRISTIAN'S SERVICE
Chapter 5

As Peter closes this letter of encouragement, he speaks about:

(a) SERVING AS A SHEPHERD
Chapter 5 verses 1-4

Peter addresses the elders – and it is important to note that they are addressed in the plural.

It is not easy to be a shepherd/pastor/elder in ordinary times, but in times of persecution there is added danger. The leaders are always hunted down.

"Feed the flock of God which is among you, taking the oversight thereof, not by constraint, but willingly; not for filthy lucre, but of a ready mind; Neither as being lords over God's heritage, but being ensamples to the flock. And when the chief Shepherd shall appear, ye shall receive a crown of glory that fadeth not away" (verses 2-4).

Can you see here the *Duty of the Shepherd?*

"Feed the flock of God which is among you."

"Feed" means: *feed – and protect, discipline, restore.*

Can you see here the *Manner of the Shepherd?*

We are to serve the flock *Effectively*: *"taking the oversight"*.
We are to serve the flock *Willingly*: *"not by constraint, but willingly"*.
We are to serve the flock *Selflessly*: *"not for filthy lucre"*.

Can you see the *Sphere of the Shepherd?*

"God's heritage!" "Heritage" means: *"lot"* for there are lots or portions entrusted to the elders, places of God's choosing.

Can you see the *Reward of the Shepherd?*

"A crown of glory."
Unlike the other crowns, this is an exclusive crown. It is reserved for those who faithfully shepherd God's flock, God's way.

Elders, is this reward not worth striving for? To hear on that day: *"Well done"* and the unfading crown of glory that goes with it.

(b) SERVING AS A SAINT
Chapter 5 verses 5-7

Peter commands all Christians to submit to each other and to the Lord.

How are we to do this?

The answer is: *"be clothed with humility"* (verse 5).

Humility is not thinking poorly of yourself. It is simply not thinking of yourself at all! (Philippians 2:5)

(c) SERVING AS A SOLDIER
Chapter 5 verses 8-14

We are in a battle against an enemy who is the accuser and the devourer (verse 8). We need to be watchful and hold our ground (verses 8-9). The roaring lion is still abroad.

"Never mind" says Peter.

"But the God of all grace, who hath called us unto His eternal glory by Christ Jesus, after that ye have suffered a while, make you perfect, stablish, strengthen, settle you" (verse 10).

What tremendous trials these believers faced!
What untold suffering they endured!
What horrible deaths they died!

Was there a crumb of comfort for them? Yes!

There was **God's Care!**

"Casting all your care upon Him; for He careth for you" (verse 7).

Or:

"Casting all your care upon Him; for you are His concern."

Did you notice that there are two cares in this verse?

There is *Anxious Care,* that is ours; but there is *Affectionate Care,* that is His.

Dr. Sidlow Baxter says:

"Think of it, He who carries the universe on His shoulders carries you and me continually on His heart."

There was **God's Control!**

These trials are purposeful. Is this not what Peter says here in verse 10? The Lord uses the fiery trials of life to give us stability and steadfastness.

Nothing touches you that has not come through the sovereign hand of the Lord.

God is always in control.

There was **God's Glory!**

"His eternal glory."

No assault from hell, no affliction on earth can hinder this wonderful consummation.

No wonder Peter breaks out in thanksgiving and says:

"To Him be glory and dominion for ever and ever. Amen" (verse 11).

"Oft times the day seems long,
Our trials hard to bear,
We're tempted to complain,
To murmur and despair;
But Christ will soon appear
To catch His bride away,
All tears forever over
In God's eternal day.

Sometimes the sky looks dark,
With not a ray of light,
We're tossed and driven on,
No human help in sight;
But there is One in Heaven,
Who knows our deepest care,
Let Jesus solve your problem –
Just go to Him in prayer.

Life's day will soon be o'er,
All storms forever past,
We'll cross the great divide,
To glory, Safe at last;
We'll share the joys of heaven,
A harp, a home, a crown,
The tempter will be banished,
We'll lay our burdens down.

> *It will be worth it all,*
> *When we see Jesus,*
> *Life's trials will seem so small,*
> *When we see Christ;*
> *One glimpse of His dear face,*
> *All sorrow will erase,*
> *So bravely run the race,*
> *Till we see Christ."*

CHAPTER 22

2 Peter

A Dr. Congdon approached Bible teacher R. A. Torrey and complained that he could get nothing out of his Bible study.

"Please tell me how to study it so that it will mean something to me."

"Read it", replied Dr. Torrey.

"I do read it", explained Dr. Congdon.

"Read it some more", advised Dr. Torrey.

"How?" Dr. Congdon asked.

"Take some book and read it twelve times a day for a month." Torrey recommended 2 Peter.

Dr. Congdon later said:

"My wife and I read 2 Peter four times in the morning, four times at noon, and four times at dinner. Soon I was talking 2 Peter to everyone I met. It seemed as though the stars in the heavens were singing the story of 2 Peter. I read 2 Peter on my knees, marking passages. Teardrops mingled with the crayon colors, and I said to my wife, 'See how I have ruined this part of my Bible.' 'Yes', she said, 'but as the pages have been getting blacker, your life has been getting whiter'."

The book of 2 Peter was an unusual book for R. A. Torrey to recommend! It has been viewed by some as the *"dark corner"* of the New Testament. As a result it is not often preached, studied, discussed or even quoted.

Yet the church of Jesus Christ ignores this epistle at its peril.

It would almost seem that 2 Peter was written specially for us at this crucial time in the Twenty-First Century.

Let us note a few things about the book that will help us in our study. Notice:

1. THE CHARACTER OF THE BOOK

The letter commences:

"Simon Peter, a servant and an apostle of Jesus Christ."

Peter, of course, was the acknowledged leader and spokesman of the apostles. As such, his name heads all the four New Testament lists of the Twelve. He dominates the Gospel records and the first part of the Acts of the Apostles.

After his appearance at the Jerusalem Council in Acts 15, Peter seems to disappear from the scene yet Scripture indicates that he was engaged in missionary travels (1 Corinthians 1:12, 1 Corinthians 9:5; Galatians 2:11-21).

One thing is certain:

(a) His Authorship is Questioned

Some commentators raise three objections to Peter's authorship of this letter. The objections are:

(1) That the early writers seldom referred to this epistle.

We can answer: The church fathers were slow in giving it their acceptance, but this also applies to some of the other writings.

(2) That the style and language of this letter is very different from the first, therefore it could not have been written by Peter.

We can answer: The differences in language and style can be explained by the differences in theme. First Peter was written to help suffering Christians, but Second Peter was written to expose false teachers. The two letters were written in different circumstances and for a different purpose, dealing with different subjects. Yet there *are* similarities between the two.

If you go through the two letters, Peter keeps using the word: *"precious"*. Everything is *"precious"* to Peter. He must have liked the word *"precious"*, for he wrote about the: *"precious faith"* (1 Peter 1:7); *"precious blood"* (1 Peter 1:19); *"precious stone"* (1 Peter 2:4, 6); *"precious Saviour"* (1 Peter 2:7); *"precious faith"* (2 Peter 1:1) and *"precious promises"* (2 Peter 1:4).

Would that not lead you to believe that it is the same man who writes these two letters?

(3) That this could not have been written in Peter's lifetime as Peter talks about Paul's epistles, and all of Paul's epistles had not been written then. (2 Peter 3:16)

We can answer: Surely the phrase: *"all his epistles"* refers to the epistles that had been written then.

This letter was written by Peter. The opening verse bears the name of Peter himself.

Still again, Peter was an eye-witness of the Transfiguration (Matthew 17:1-9) – and the writer describes himself as such in Chapter 1 verse 16.

In addition, in Chapter 3 verse 1, it states that Peter had written the previous letter to the same people.

And:

(b) His End is Near

Do you see what Peter says in Chapter 1 verse 14?

"Knowing that shortly I must put off this my tabernacle, even as our Lord Jesus Christ hath shewed me."

Do you recall what is recorded in John's Gospel? The Risen Lord said to Peter:

"When thou wast young, thou girdest thyself, and walkedst whither thou wouldest: but when thou shalt be old, thou shalt stretch forth thy hands, and another shall gird thee, and carry thee whither thou wouldest not" (John 21:18).

In verse 19, John then gives the interpretation:

"This spake He, signifying by what death he should glorify God."

Peter was going to die as our Lord died - on a cross. Tradition tells us that this is exactly what happened. He had the grim ordeal of seeing his wife suffer before him. Then, when they came to take him, Peter said:

"Crucify me with my head downwards. My Master was crucified for me with His head upwards. I am not worthy to die as He died."

Peter was martyred around 68 A.D. He wrote his first letter around 64-65 A.D. and possibly this letter shortly before his death.

Thus 2 Peter and 2 Timothy have much in common.

Both books are the last written by their authors.

Both contain a passage on the subject of inspiration – 2 Peter 1 verse 20 and 2 Timothy 3 verse 16.

Both warn against apostasy - 2 Peter 2 and 2 Timothy 3.

Both men knew that they would die a martyr's death – 2 Peter 1 verses 13 to 15 and 2 Timothy 4 verse 6.

So here is Peter, perhaps in prison, with his death imminent, writing to these believers who lived in a far-flung region of the Roman Empire covering the area now belonging to Turkey.

What is Peter's concern as he writes this letter?

2. THE CONTRAST OF THE BOOK

What a contrast this letter is from the first one! You see, this letter deals with a totally different situation from the first one. The readers are the same and it is a few years later but now Peter feels the urgent need to address *dangers within the church.*

There are two kinds of pressures that churches always face.

Dangers from without and dangers from within.

In 1 Peter, we see Satan as a roaring lion seeking to devour. Peter's theme is persecution.
In 2 Peter, we see Satan as a serpent seeking to deceive. Peter's theme is heresy.

Which do you think is the more dangerous?

Fierce persecution from without or false teaching from within?

Do you recall that when Paul was saying goodbye to the elders at Ephesus he warned them?

"For I know this, that after my departing shall grievous wolves enter in among you, not sparing the flock. Also of your own selves shall men arise, speaking perverse things, to draw away disciples after them" (Acts 20:29-30).

The danger from without and the danger from within.

Satan has never destroyed the church with persecution. In fact, the harder he hits, the more the church seems to grow and prosper. *I mean, where in this world is the church of Jesus Christ the strongest?* Is it not in those lands where persecution is rife? China, India, the Far East, Iran! *The blood of the martyrs is indeed the seed of the church!* Persecution cleanses the church and strengthens the church. But, is pressure from within not more dangerous?

While hostility was the theme of the first letter, heresy is the theme of the second letter.

The first letter dealt with trials from without (1 Peter 1:6-7).
The second letter is enemies from within (2 Peter 2:1).

The first letter was a letter of consolation, the second letter is a letter of warning.
The first is all about encouragement for the church, the second is all about error in the church.
The first letter dealt with the subject of pain, but the second letter deals with the subject of poison.

Peter was facing impending martyrdom, but his main concern was that after his departure heresy could creep into the church and lead the flock of God astray.

Then you need to see:

3. THE CONCLUSION OF THE BOOK

What is Peter's judgment as he writes this letter? Just this:

The primary solution to false teaching is knowledge of true doctrine.

The words *"know"* or *"knowledge"* are used at least thirteen times in this short letter. Those words do not mean a mere intellectual understanding of some truth, although that is included. It means a living participation in the truth.

This is the sense that Christ used it in John 17 verse 3:

"And this is life eternal, that they might know Thee the only true God, and Jesus Christ, whom Thou hast sent."

It is an experiential knowledge of God, based on the Scriptures.

Is this not why the Word of God is so central in this book? The only weapon to fight false teaching and the lies of the devil is the Word of God. This is why Peter emphasizes spiritual knowledge. There are three chapters in this little letter and three words sum up these three chapters.

The first chapter is all about Consolation.
The second chapter is about Condemnation.
The third chapter is about Consummation.

1. CONSOLIDATION
Chapter 1

"To consolidate" is: *"to make or become stronger".*

Is this not Peter's desire for these believers?

The theme of the first letter is *grace;* the theme of the second letter is *knowledge.* Peter sums up both books by exhorting us to: *"Grow in grace, and in the knowledge of our Lord and Saviour Jesus Christ"* (2 Peter 3:18).

We need to have Bible truth in our heads (*knowledge*) and we need to show Bible truth in our lives (*grace*).

We need to learn and to live the Word.

This opening section is all about faith. Peter talks about:

(a) THE GIFT OF FAITH
Chapter 1 verses 1-4

The letter commences:

"Simon Peter, a servant and an apostle of Jesus Christ, to them that have obtained like precious faith with us through the righteousness of God and our Saviour Jesus Christ."

"Obtained like precious faith."

Is faith not a gift?

In Ephesians 2 verse 8, Paul says:
"For by grace are ye saved through faith; and that not of yourselves: it is the gift of God."

You see, this faith:

Identifies us with a Divine Person

Can you see **His Deity?**

"God and our Saviour" are not two different persons! Rather, both terms refer to the same person. Peter is not just identifying Christ as Saviour but as God (see also Titus 2:10 and Chapter 3:4).

Can you see **His Ability?**

"And our Saviour Jesus Christ." A Saviour is one who brings salvation. When we put our faith in Him, He gives us righteousness, grace and peace. Indeed, we become: *"partakers of the divine nature"* (2 Peter 1:4). That is, partakers in the very life that belongs to God (Colossians 3:3 and 1 John 5:11).

Identifies us with a Divine Company

Peter calls it: *"to them that have obtained like precious faith"* or: *"to those who have a faith the same kind as ours"* (2 Peter 1:1).

It means that our standing with the Lord today is the same as that of the apostles centuries ago. They had no special advantage over us simply because they were privileged to walk with Christ. Christians today are tempted to think of the apostles as mighty men of superhuman faith. But God sees no distinction among Christians.

As Paul says:

"There is neither Jew nor Greek, there is neither bond nor free, there is neither male nor female: for ye are all one in Christ Jesus" (Galatians 3:28).

Identifies us with Divine Resources

"According as His divine power hath given unto us all things that pertain unto life and godliness, through the knowledge of Him that hath called us to glory and virtue" (verse 3).

We have Divine Power

Whatever sufficiency we have is not because of any power we possess in ourselves but *"according to the power that worketh in us"* (Ephesians 3:20).

We have Divine Provision

"All things that pertain unto life and godliness."

When you are born into the family of God, you are born complete. What is true in the natural realm is true in the spiritual realm. A baby is born complete.

A lot of Christians do not believe that. They are always looking for something more: some new experience, some new truth, some further revelation, some elevating emotional high. Do you know people like that? They are seeking *"second blessings"*, *"Spirit baptisms"*, tongues, mystical experiences, private revelations, the *"deeper life"* in an attempt to attain what is supposed to be missing from their lives.

Do you hear what Peter says?

"You do not need any new experience or revelation. You already have everything you need to be able to serve, to please and to imitate the Lord."

Is this not an amazing statement?

If something is missing in your life, it is **not because you need any more of Christ. It may be that Christ needs more of you.**

We have Divine Promises

"Whereby are given unto us exceeding great and precious promises" (verse 4).

What are these *"exceeding great and precious promises"*?

The glorious doctrinal facts presented in the Word of God.

In other words, God has given us His Word to develop this life and godliness.

This is all enshrined in the gift of faith.

(b) THE GROWTH OF FAITH
Chapter 1 verses 5-11

Do you see what Peter says?

"And beside this, giving all diligence, add ..."

This indicates there is something beyond the new birth. There is growth!

A wife became quite concerned over her husband's declining health. His colour was very pale. He had a terrible lack of energy for even the simplest of tasks. After much prodding, she persuaded him to go to the doctor to find out what his problem might be. The doctor examined him carefully and ran tests to determine the exact natures of the man's illness. After evaluating the test results, he called the woman into his office to give his prognosis.

"Your husband is suffering from a rare form of anemia. Without proper treatment, he could be dead in a matter of just a few weeks", he informed the very anxious wife.

He went on to say:
"However, it can be successfully treated with the right care and diet. With the proper course of treatment, I am happy to report that you can expect full recovery."

The wife was very relieved and asked what kind of action was necessary.

The doctor gave his prescription:
"You will need to get up every morning and fix a complete breakfast of pancakes, eggs, bacon, etc. Make sure that he has a home-cooked lunch each afternoon of fresh-baked bread and homemade soup. For dinner, prepare a meal of fresh salad, old-fashioned meat and potatoes, fresh vegetables and perhaps homemade pie or cake for dessert. Because his immune system is so compromised, you will need to keep the house scrupulously clean. It will also be important to keep his stress level very low, so avoid any kind of confrontation or argument."

The wife emerged from the doctor's office and with tears rolling down her cheeks, she faced her husband.

The husband took one look at his wife and said very seriously:
"The news is bad, isn't it? What did the doctor say?"

With a choked voice, the sobbing wife told her beloved husband:
"The doctor says that you're going to die!"

Growth as a Christian should not be something we see as optional. It is something we must spend the rest of our life doing. It is like riding a bicycle uphill. If you stop pedalling, you are going to go backwards.

The Christian life is not a static experience. We have to be growing. It is not enough to be born into the family of God. We need to grow spiritually. This demands diligence and earnestness.

How were you at mathematics at school?

This chapter has been called: *"the mathematics chapter"*.

There is *Multiplication*: *"Grace and peace be multiplied unto you"* (verse 2).
There is *Addition*: *"Add to your faith"* (verse 5).
There is *Subtraction*: *"he was purged from his old sins"* (verse 9).

Peter now lists seven qualities the believer is to expand and develop:

Virtue: it means *"excellence"*. A Christian is supposed to glorify the Lord because he has God's nature within and when he does this he shows *"excellence"*.

Knowledge: a reference to moral discernment. This, of course, comes from studying the Word.

Temperance: it means self-control (Proverbs 16:32 and Chapter 25:28).

Patience: the ability to endure when life is difficult.

Godliness: means *"God-likeness"*. A reverence and a fear of God and respect for His people.

Brotherly kindness: that must have be hard for Peter, for the disciples, like us, often disagreed with one another.

Charity: a love for saints, sinners, the servants of God, the Scriptures and the Saviour.

Do you see the result of all this?

"For if these things be in you, and abound, they make you that ye shall neither be barren nor unfruitful in the knowledge of our Lord Jesus Christ" (verse 8).

Stunted growth, by contrast, means idleness and fruitlessness and blindness (verse 9).

Ray Stedman asked a boy how old he was. Quick as a flash, the boy said: *"I'm twelve, going on thirteen, soon be fourteen."* That boy was eager to grow up!

Most of us want to grow in the Lord, especially when we are new in the faith. But often, as time goes on, the enthusiasm to grow begins to fade. We settle into a humdrum routine and grow spiritually complacent.

Steven Cole tells about an old farmer who often described his Christian experience by saying:
"Well, I'm not making much progress, but I'm established!"

One Spring, when he was hauling some logs, his wagon wheels sank down to the axles in mud. As he sat there, viewing the dismal situation, a neighbour who had always felt uncomfortable with the farmer's worn-out testimony came by.

He called out:
"Brother Jones, I see you're not making much progress, but you must be content because you're well established."

It was a way of pointing out: *"You're stuck!"*

Let me ask: Is that you? Are you stuck?

No growth? No development? No progress?

Well, Peter says: *"Be diligent!"*

Be sure you are saved! Ensure that you have the marks of a true believer.

(c) THE GROUND OF FAITH
Chapter 1 verses 12-21

How can we be so sure that this message is the true Word of God?

Peter answers that question by speaking about:

A Sensational Wonder

Do you see verses 15 to 17?

"Moreover I will endeavour that ye may be able after my decease to have

these things always in remembrance. For we have not followed cunningly devised fables, when we made known unto you the power and coming of our Lord Jesus Christ, but were eyewitnesses of His majesty. For He received from God the Father honour and glory, when there came such a voice to Him from the excellent glory, This is My beloved Son, in whom I am well pleased."

What is Peter talking about? He is referring to his experience with Christ on the Mount of Transfiguration. This experience is recorded by Matthew in Chapter 17 of his Gospel, by Mark in Chapter 9 of his Gospel and by Luke in Chapter 9 of his Gospel. Yet, none of those men actually participated in it. But Peter did. Indeed, the words that he uses in this passage remind us of his experience *"in the holy mount"*.

Look at verses 13 and 14 where he uses the word *"tabernacle"* on two occasions.

Do you recall what he said on the Mountain? *"Lord, it is good for us to be here; ... let us make here three tabernacles; one for Thee, and one for Moses, and one for Elias"* (Matthew 17:4).

But what was the significance of the Transfiguration?

Well, it was a picture of the coming kingdom which these false teachers were denying (2 Peter 3:4).

You see, in all three Gospels where the account of the Transfiguration is recorded, it is introduced with a statement about the kingdom. For example, here is Luke 9 verse 27:

"But I tell you of a truth, there be some standing here, which shall not taste of death, till they see the kingdom of God."

This is just prior to the Transfiguration.

Moreover, the word *"kingdom"* can be translated: *"royal splendour"*.

Do you see what Christ was promising? That before they died, some of the disciples would see the kingdom of God in power! When did that happen? A few days later, on the Mount of Transfiguration, when the Lord Jesus revealed His glory.

The question had been raised:
"What about God's promises to the Jews of a glorious kingdom on earth?"

Well, Peter is saying:
"We have Christ's Transfiguration to assure us that the kingdom will come."

The glory that was revealed on the Mount will be the glory that will be displayed at Christ's Second Coming.

The false teachers denied the promise of His Coming and substituted God's promises with *"cunningly devised fables"* (verse 16) that robbed the Christians of their blessed hope. But Peter says: *"I was there with Christ on the Mount. I was an eye-witness of His Majesty"*.

Peter was there and he recorded his experience for us in this letter that he wrote inspired by the Spirit of God. Experiences fade, but the Word of God remains and so Peter passes from a sensational wonder to:

A Sure Word

As helpful and reliable as Peter's experience was, the prophetic word of Scripture is more sure. Peter says in verse 19: *"We have also a more sure word of prophecy"*.

More sure than what? Than experience! Peter was saying, in effect, that although the Transfiguration was a wonderful experience, Scripture was a more trustworthy verification of his faith.

Though he had seen no less than the Lord in His glory, Peter was certain that the Word of God recorded by holy men moved by the Holy Spirit was a more solid foundation for what he believed.

Can you see here?

The Importance of God's Word

"A more sure word of prophecy." Is this not the problem with many today? They want a *"charismatic"* experience, usually something extra-biblical. They want voices and visions, sounds and signs, revelations and rantings. Is this not the major flaw in the Charismatic movement? It calls on experience rather than the Word of God to tell us what is true. Your experience or my experience or someone else's experience! But where does Peter turn us? He takes us back to the Book.

Here is the basis of our belief. Here is the ground of our faith. The Bible, the Word of God.

Is this not where we need to turn when heresy, apostasy and error invade the church?

The Interpretation of God's Word

"Knowing this first, that no prophecy of the Scripture is of any private interpretation" (verse 20).

For a long time, the Church of Rome used this text to support the idea that no-one could come privately or personally to the Bible to interpret it. He had to have the interpretation of the church. But that is not what this means. The word *"private"* means: *"by itself"* or *"individually"*. It is simply saying that no verse in the Bible should be interpreted in and of itself, apart from the whole of God's divine revelation. In other words, we do not interpret one Scripture in a way that contradicts another Scripture.

It is still true that *a text taken out of context is a pretext*.

The Inspiration of God's Word

The Bible did not come by the will of man. Rather, Scripture comes from God (verse 21). The most important word here is: *"moved"*.

This speaks of being carried along by the Holy Spirit, as a ship is carried by the wind. You see, these men wrote as the Spirit of God directed them to write and what they wrote was in a very real sense not their words, it was the very Word of God.

Our Bible is true! We can trust it because God gave it to us and it is the ground of our faith.

2. CONDEMNATION
Chapter 2

Peter speaks of false teachers who bring in *"damnable"* heresies. The word: *"damnable"* means: *"utter ruin"*. There will be eternal condemnation for false teachers and their followers.

Peter is saying: *"Beware of counterfeits!"*

The nation of Israel was constantly being led astray by false prophets. Do you recall that Elijah (1 Kings 18:22), Isaiah (Isaiah 9:15 and Chapter 28:7) and Jeremiah (Jeremiah 14:14) had to contend with false prophets? Moreover, our Lord Jesus, in His discourses, gave warning of these things. Do you recall Christ's words?

"Beware of false prophets, which come to you in sheep's clothing, but inwardly they are ravening wolves" (Matthew 7:15).

"Many false prophets shall rise, and shall deceive many" (Matthew 24:11).

Peter touches here on:

(a) The Doctrine of these False Teachers
Chapter 2 verses 1-3

The term *"heresies"*, according to W.E. Vine, denotes: *"an opinion especially a self-willed opinion, which is substituted to the power of truth and leads to division and the formation of sects"*.

These false teachers had exchanged the truth of God's Word for their own self-styled opinions.

Peter points out that they teach destructive heresies.

They *Denied the Saviour* (verse 1).
They *Decried the Scriptures* (verse 2).
They *Derided the Second Coming of the Lord Jesus* (2 Peter 3:1-4).

Do you know what Peter's response to false teaching is? *A knowledge of the truth.* He longs that we be: *"established in the present truth"* (2 Peter 1:12).

The spirit of the age is doctrinal compromise. We are told that we must learn to worship, witness, and work together, whether we be Protestant or Catholic, evangelical or liberal, charismatic or conservative, but Peter's position is entirely different. *He says we have to fight for the faith.*

(b) The Doom of these False Teachers
Chapter 2 verses 4-9

False teachers will be ultimately condemned by God. Peter cites three Old Testament examples to prove it: the angels that sinned and are now imprisoned (verse 4), the flood (verse 5) and the cities of Sodom and Gomorrah (verses 6-9).

What a contrast between the false teachers and the authentic believers

We are not looking for judgment but for the coming of the Lord to take us home to glory. These false teachers, however, are doomed.

(c) The Deeds of these False Teachers
Chapter 2 verses 10-17

Alan Cairns says:

"False prophets are always unscriptural in their doctrine and usually unclean in their lives."

What a catalogue of sin is brought before us here.
   They were proud – verses 10-11.
   They were ignorant – verse 12.
   They were lustful – verses 13-14.
   They were covetous – verses 15-16.

They thought that it did not matter how they lived. They supposed they had a ticket to heaven, but surely people who make grace a covering for sin are strangers to grace!

(d) The Deception of these False Teachers
Chapter 2 verses 18-22

They promise liberty but lead people into bondage.
They are the blind leading the blind (Matthew 15:14).
They are as filthy pigs and dogs.

Some people wonder whether Peter is teaching here that a Christian can lose his salvation?

Not on your life!

Nowhere in the Bible does the Lord call a Christian a pig or a dog. Rather, Peter compares us to sheep (1 Peter 2:25). These are false teachers going back to the life that suited their nature (2 Peter 2:21-22).

Is this not the day we live in? A day of false teachers.

Warren Wiersbe says:
"You can detect them by their exaltation of self; their emphasis on making money; their great claims that they can change people, and their hidden lives of lust and sin."

Peter says: *"Beware!"* (2 Peter 3:17)

Watch what you are looking at on the God channel, on the internet, and on social media.

" Beware!"

3. CONSUMMATION
Chapter 3

Peter directs our minds to the Second Advent of Jesus Christ.

He says in effect: *"Remember Christ is returning and He will set matters right!"*

Of course, the devil continually places skeptics and false teachers and heretics within the church who reject, minimize or alter the promise of Christ's return.

(a) The Lord's Return is Attacked
Chapter 3 verses 1-4

The doctrine that Peter is defending here is the return of Christ to the earth to set up His kingdom, and then, after a 1000 years to usher in the new heavens and earth.

Does the world scoff at the idea of the return of Christ?

Of course! The world says: *"God is not going to break into history and interrupt the progress of time."* But God is!

Indeed here we see that:

(b) The Lord's Return is Attested
Chapter 3 verses 5-10

God did intervene in history. There was the work of God in creation (verse 5) and there was the flood in Noah's day (verse 6). God intervened in the past and He will intervene again. *"The Day of the Lord"*, that period known as the Great Tribulation, will come. It will come after the church has been raptured to heaven (Revelation 3:10), then judgment will follow.

It is interesting that Peter speaks here of three worlds. Did you notice them?

"The world that then was" (verse 6) - that is the **Past World**.

"The heavens and the earth which are now" (verse 7) - that is **the Present World**.

"Nevertheless we ... look for new heavens and a new earth" (verse 13) - that is **the Prospective World**.

(c) The Lord's Return is Applied
Chapter 3 verses 11-18

In light of the Lord's future intervention in this world, how should we live?

We need to be marked by godliness (verse 11), by holiness (verse 14), by awareness (verse 14) and by steadfastness (verse 17).

In light of His coming, do you not want to finish well?

At the 1968 Olympics in Mexico City, the last of the marathon runners were being carried off the field to first aid stations about an hour after the winner had crossed the finish line. Just a few spectators remained in the stands when they suddenly heard the sound of sirens and police whistles. All eyes turned to the gate to see John Stephen Akhwari, wearing the colours of Tanzania, limping into the stadium. His leg was bloodied and bandaged from a bad fall. He hobbled around the track past the finish line as the crowd rose and applauded as if he were the winner.

Someone later asked him why he had not quit, in view of his injury and the fact that he had no chance of winning a medal.

He replied:

"My country did not send me 7,000 miles to start the race. They sent me 7,000 miles to finish it."

Christ did not give His life for you just to start the Christian life. He gave His life so that you would finish it and finish it well.

You will do so if you guard yourself from spiritual error, grow in the grace and knowledge of Him, and live to glorify His name.

CHAPTER 23
1 John

John was now a very old man, feeling the weight of his years and aware that his days on earth were about done. A godly life lay behind him and a very long memory thrilled him. His native land was far away in the land of Israel. He now lived in Ephesus, a pagan Asiatic city, on the edge of the European world.

1. THE AUTHOR OF THIS BOOK

Although the letter does not identify the author, the earliest testimony of the church ascribes it to John. Not only one of the Twelve, he was one of the three most intimate associates of Christ, along with Peter and James (Mark 5:37; Chapter 9:2 and Chapter 14:33). He was an eyewitness to and a participant in Christ's earthly ministry (1 John 1:1-4).

Dr. Graham Scroggie remarks:

"John was the first to appear on the stage of apostolic story and he was the last to leave it. In matter of years he spans the first century."

This John, the beloved disciple, is the author of 5 books of the New Testament. Apart from Paul, no other author would write as much sacred Scripture in the New Testament as he did.

John gave us the Gospel of John, 1 John, 2 John, and 3 John, and the book of Revelation.

These 5 books are in three main groups.

First is the Gospel, which has to do with *our past,* and deals with the theme *of salvation.*

The three epistles have to do with *our present* and deal with the theme *of sanctification.*

The last book in the Bible deals with *our future* and the theme is *glorification.*

Now it is characteristic of John in his writings to put a key either at the front door or the back door of the book. For example, in the book of Revelation, the key is hanging at the front door. In Revelation 1 verse 19, John was told by the Lord: *"Write the things which thou hast seen, and the things which are, and the things which shall be hereafter".* Now that simple outline is the key to understanding the book of Revelation. In his Gospel, John puts the key at the back door. He says: *"These are written, that ye might believe that Jesus is the Christ, the Son of God; and that believing ye might have life through His name"* (John 20:31). So the Gospel of John was written so that people might come to know the Lord who is God manifest in flesh.

Each time that John wrote a book, he always had a definite purpose in mind. So what is:

2. THE AIM OF THIS BOOK

We do not have to guess why John wrote this first epistle! In this letter there are four keys, all identified by the phrase: *"these things I write".* These provide the four reasons why John wrote this letter. John wrote:

(a) To Provide Assurance

Look at Chapter 5 verse 13:

"These things have I written unto you that believe on the name of the Son of God; that ye may know that ye have eternal life, and that ye may believe on the name of the Son of God."

This word *"know"* should be circled in your Bible. It is the key word in 1 John for it is used over 30 times.

Some say: *"Well, you cannot really know that you are going to heaven when you die!"*
Yet John says: *"You can!"*

John is writing to provide assurance for the child of God.

Are you sure of your salvation?

Dr. Martyn Lloyd-Jones said: *"Assurance is not essential to salvation, but it is essential to the joy of salvation".*

(b) To Protect Believers

Look at Chapter 2 verse 26:

"These things have I written unto you concerning them that seduce you."

John's purpose is to protect the saints from those who would lead them astray. Do you recall what Paul said when he was saying: *"Farewell!"* to the elders at Ephesus?

"For I know this, that after my departing shall grievous wolves enter in among you, not sparing the flock. Also of your own selves shall men arise, speaking perverse things, to draw away disciples after them" (Acts 20:29-30).

As the First Century drew to a close, outward hostility was giving way to inward corruption. False teachers from within the church's own ranks began infecting the church with false doctrine. This teaching eventually became known as: *"Gnosticism"*, with the word coming from the Greek word *"gnosis"*, meaning: *"to know"*. The word *"agnostic"* means: *"someone who does not know"*. Therefore, a *"gnostic"* was a *"religious know-it-all"*. The Gnostics believed that all matter was evil. This meant that the body was evil, that the flesh was evil and that anything material or physical was evil. Therefore, they denied the humanity of Christ. They were going around saying that Jesus Christ was not human at all. He just appeared to be human. He was a phantom. Others, like a man called Cerinthus, said that Jesus was a human being and that the divine Christ came upon Him at His baptism and departed before His crucifixion.

They did not believe in the incarnation, the literal coming into human existence of the Lord Jesus. Does doctrine matter? Of course it does! Deny the humanity of Christ and you will have to deny the work of Christ, and if you deny the work of Christ, then there is no salvation.

> *"What think ye of Christ? is the test,*
> *To try both your state and your scheme,*
> *You cannot be right in the rest,*
> *Unless you think rightly of Him."*

There are always going to be people who will attack the Lord Jesus. They will attack Him from all sides. They will either attack His deity or else they will attack His humanity.

John is thus writing to protect the saints.

(c) To Prevent Sin

Look at Chapter 2 verse 1:

"My little children, these things write I unto you, that ye sin not. And if any man sin, we have an advocate with the Father, Jesus Christ the righteous."

The Bible nowhere teaches that a Christian is sinless, but it does teach that a child of God ought to sin less. Day by day we ought to grow in grace and sin less today, than we did yesterday.

(d) To Promote Joy

Look at Chapter 1 verse 4:

"These things write we unto you, that your joy may be full."

So John is writing to promote joy in the heart of the child of God.

Do you have joy today? Are you happy in the Lord?

3. THE ANALYSIS

Many Bible scholars have said that this letter is impossible to analyse because John seems to go round in circles. His letter has been compared to a spiral staircase because John keeps returning to the same three topics of *obedience* (1 John 1:5-2:29 and Chapter 3:1-24); *love* (1 John 2:7-17 and Chapter 4:1-21) and *truth* (1 John 2:18-29 and Chapter 5:1-21). John picks up a word or a thought, then puts it down, only to pick it up again. The three prominent words of the Gospel of John are emphasised here again, *Light, Love, and Life.*

John knows no shades of grey. Things are either right or wrong, true or false, good or bad, black or white. John speaks of life and death, truth and falsehood, love and hate, light and darkness, righteousness and sin, the Father and the World, children of God and children of the Devil.

We will shortly divide John's book into three parts, but this may not be that satisfactory.

As John Phillips says:

"We get the feeling that John would have recognised no such analysis at all."

4. THE AUDIENCE

To whom is John writing?

It is believed by some that John directed his epistles to the same readers who would later receive the book of Revelation, that is the seven churches in Asia Minor. No doubt there is a measure of truth in this. This letter was probably written from Ephesus about 90 A.D. perhaps designed first of all for the church of Ephesus, then for the churches of Asia (modern day Turkey) and, finally, for the whole church of God, for all Christian believers everywhere.

John's letter is vitally important. It gives us guidance on what a real Christian is. John says, in a world of make believe, in a world where absolutes are out of fashion, in a world of fantasy, in a world of shallow relationships, in a world of so many shades of grey: *"Be real, be authentic!"*

As already mentioned, John's great words are: Light, Love and Life.

(1) GOD IS LIGHT
Chapter 1 - Chapter 2

Do you see the simple statement in Chapter 1 verse 5?

"This then is the message which we have heard of Him, and declare unto you, that God is light, and in Him is no darkness at all."

This is the basis of our *fellowship.*

Later on, John makes another statement about God. He says: *"God is love"* (1 John 4:8).

That is the basis of our *sonship.*

So, it is possible for us to be sons of God because God is love and it is possible for us to have fellowship with God because God is light.

Now, John does not say that God has a light or God is a light. No! *God in His nature is light.* God's essence, His very being, is light.

Do you recall the words of the Psalmist?
"The Lord is my light and my salvation" (Psalm 27:1).

Writing to young Timothy, Paul describes God: *"who only hath immortality, dwelling in the light which no man can approach unto"* (1 Timothy 6:16).

When John says: *"God is light"*, he is speaking:

Physically of the Glory of God (Genesis 1:3 and Exodus 13:21).
Intellectually of the Knowledge of the God (Job 36:4 and Psalm 73:11).
Morally of the Holiness of God.

John is making a statement about the character of God. He is saying that God is absolutely holy, God is totally moral. Nothing whatsoever in God is wrong (James 1:13).

Thomas Binney put it like this:

> *"Eternal Light! Eternal Light!*
> *How pure that soul must be*
> *When, placed within Thy searching sight,*
> *It shrinks not, but with calm delight*
> *Can live and look on Thee."*

How can we live in that light? How can we have fellowship with God?

The word *"fellowship"* is the Greek word: *"koinonia"*.

A teacher in her Sunday School class said: *"Can anyone tell me what fellowship is?"*
One little boy raised his hand and said: *"It is two fellows in the same ship!"*
Not quite!
The Greek word means: *"to have in common"*, *"to share something together"*.

Do you see what John says?

"And truly our fellowship is with the Father, and with His Son Jesus Christ" (1 John 1:3).

Does that not stagger your imagination?
You can have fellowship with God!

You can be as close to God as two friends walking down a country lane.

John speaks here about:

(a) The Beginning of this Fellowship
Chapter 1 verses 1-4

The source of this fellowship!

Look at the first two verses:

"That which was from the beginning, which we have heard, which we have seen with our eyes, which we have looked upon, and our hands have handled, of the Word of life; (For the life was manifested, and we have seen it, and bear witness, and shew unto you that eternal life, which was with the Father, and was manifested unto us)."

The beginning of *"living in the light"* is historical.

It begins with Christ, the One who had dwelt in that light from all eternity and who was born at Bethlehem.

In this opening statement, John plunges right into the Gnostic controversy. In this letter, he warns us several times not to listen to false teachers who tell lies about Christ (1 John 2:22 and Chapter 4:2-3). If a man is wrong about Jesus Christ, he is wrong about God, because the Lord Jesus is the final and complete revelation of God to man. John describes Him as: *"the Word of life"*. The Lord Jesus is God's communication to us. He reveals to us the mind and heart of God.

Do you see how John describes Christ?

He speaks of Christ Eternally:

"That which was from the beginning."

"From the beginning." In his Gospel, John goes further back by saying: *"In the beginning"*.

Do you see the difference?

The Lord Jesus was in the beginning. The Lord Jesus was from the beginning. Therefore, Christ is eternal. There was never a time when He was not nor is there a time when He will not be.

The Lord Jesus is co-equal, co-eternal and co-existent with God.

Then John speaks of Christ Historically:

The word for *"manifested"* means: *"to be made visible"*.

The eternal Christ was born, became visible and lived and moved on this earth (1 Timothy 3:16). Do you see that John appeals to three of the senses that identify a person as a real person? He says: *"we heard"*, then he uses the word: *"seen"*, then he uses the word: *"handled"*. What it means is: *"we touched Him"* (Luke 24:39).

Why was John at pains to establish the perfect humanity of Christ? To counteract this heresy of Gnosticism.

The cultists were going around saying that Jesus Christ was not human at all. He just appeared to be human. He was a phantom.

But John says:

"Nonsense! Of course He was real. I was there. I heard Him, saw Him and touched Him. I know."

Do you notice that John speaks of Christ Relationally?

John uses a lovely phrase when he talks about: *"that eternal life, which was with the Father"*. Here is someone unique, someone who shared eternity with God in a most extraordinary way. Yet John says: *"He appeared"*.

It is interesting that John wrote his Gospel to prove the Deity of the Lord Jesus, then he writes his epistle to prove the Humanity of Christ.

Are you not glad that Christ was: *"made in the likeness of men"* (Philippians 2:7)? That Jesus Christ was a real man? Because of that, He can be touched with the feeling of your infirmity.

(b) The Basis of this Fellowship
Chapter 1 verses 5-7

God is light. Sin is darkness. We have to walk in the light. We cannot live in light and darkness at the same time. Now it is possible that there were some in Ephesus who started to believe that you could walk in spiritual and moral darkness and still have fellowship with God. People were living in sin and claiming that they were in fellowship with God.

John says: *"Impossible!"*

Someone has said:
"You might just as well live in a coal pit and claim that you are developing a sun tan."

It is crazy! It is impossible!

Do you claim to live in fellowship with God? Then, are you walking in the light? Are you walking in holiness of life?

Can you see:

(c) The Breaking of this Fellowship
Chapter 1 verse 8 to Chapter 2 verse 2

What is it that breaks fellowship with God in the life of a believer? **Sin.** You see, some of the false teachers were claiming that they had attained a life of sinless perfection, but John says they are liars.

"If we say that we have no sin, we deceive ourselves, and the truth is not in us" (1 John 1:8).

Though it is true that a Christian does not have to sin, it simply is not true that a Christian will never again sin. In Philippians 3 verse 12, Paul declares: *"Not as though I had already attained, either were already perfect"*.

When the Lord saves you, He does not make you perfect. He just makes you forgiven.

Can a Christian sin? Yes.
If a Christian sins, can he lose his salvation? No.

If we do sin then we have *the victorious death of Christ to maintain our forgiveness by God*:

"The blood of Jesus Christ His Son cleanseth us from all sin" (1 John 1:7).

We also have *the victorious life of Christ to maintain our fellowship with God*:

"If any man sin, we have an advocate with the Father, Jesus Christ the righteous" (1 John 2:1).

Do you see the word *"advocate"*? It is *"parakletos"* which means: *"one called alongside to plead our case"*.

Let me give you a mental picture of what is being described here. The book of Revelation describes Satan as: *"the accuser of the brethren"* (Revelation 12:10 and Job 1:6-12). He accuses us before God day and night.

I can imagine that when we sin, Satan rushes into the presence of God and says:

"Look what he or she did. You call them 'Your child'! Just look at what they have done."

Then the Lord Jesus says:

"Yes, Father, but look at Me. On the basis of My shed blood, I plead for the remission of that sin."

You see, the Accuser is met by the Advocate. All Christ has to do is raise His pierced hands and Satan is silenced. That is how effective Christ's finished work is. What He pleads on our behalf in Heaven is the on-going effects of His own death.

> "Though the restless foe accuses -
> Sins recounting like a flood,
> Every charge our God refuses
> Christ has answered with His blood."

We thank God for the: *"finished work of Christ"* - Christ giving His life as a sacrifice for sin.
But, today He has an *"unfinished work"* in glory, as He represents us before the throne of God.

Is He not a wonderful Saviour?

Surely we should cry: *"Hallelujah, what a Saviour!"*

Did you notice:

(d) The Beauty of this Fellowship
Chapter 2 verses 3-14

Whether we are: *"little children"*, *"fathers"* or *"young men"*, we are in the family and as such should be living a life of obedience (verse 4), a life of Christlikeness (verse 6) and a life of love (verses 9-10).

John introduces us to one of his distinctive threads in this passage when he says on three occasions: *"He that saith"* (verse 4, 6 and 9).

John is using it to bring before us a series of tests by which we can know beyond any shadow of doubt that we are a child of God.

The story is told about a pious church member who thought he was a great Christian. One Sunday he visited the junior class of the Sunday School. The Superintendent asked him to say a few words to the boys and girls. He pompously stood before them and asked: *"Why do you think people call me a great Christian?"* From the back of the room, a little boy shouted out: *"Because they don't know you!"*

When you think of what a believer should be, what comes to your mind?

John brings before us here:

The Test of Loyalty: the test of faithfulness to the Word:

"And hereby we do know that we know Him, if we keep His commandments. He that saith, I know Him, and keepeth not His commandments, is a liar, and the truth is not in him. But whoso keepeth His word, in him verily is the love of God perfected: hereby know we that we are in Him" (1 John 2:3-5).

The Test of Living: the test of Christlikeness:

"He that saith he abideth in Him ought himself also so to walk, even as He walked. Brethren, I write no new commandment unto you, but an old commandment which ye had from the beginning. The old commandment is the word which ye have heard from the beginning. Again, a new commandment I write unto you, which thing is true in Him and in you: because the darkness is past, and the true light now shineth" (1 John 2:6-8).

The Test of Love:

"He that saith he is in the light, and hateth his brother, is in darkness even until now. He that loveth his brother abideth in the light, and there is none occasion of stumbling in him. But he that hateth his brother is in darkness, and walketh in darkness, and knoweth not whither he goeth, because that darkness hath blinded his eyes" (1 John 2:9-11).

If I know Him, I will want to obey Him.
If I know Him, I will want to be like Him.
If I know Him, I will want to love as He loved.

However there are:

(e) The Barriers to this Fellowship
   Chapter 2 verses 15-29

In Chapter 2 verses 15 to 17, there is the *Barrier of Worldliness*.

John is using the word *"world"* here to refer to the invisible spiritual system of evil.

So what is worldliness?
John Wesley says: *"Anything that cools my love for Christ is the world"*.

What is worldliness?
It is anything that keeps me from loving the Lord as I ought to love Him and from doing the will of God as I ought to do it.

Worldliness is primarily living to experience the world's passing pleasures.

Do you know anything about it?
Has worldliness infiltrated into your life?

In Chapter 2 verse 18 to 27, there is the *Barrier of Falseness*.

John speaks about the false teachers. Do you see in verse 19 the sharp contrast between: *"they"* and *"us"*? False teachers and true believers!

John says that false teachers:
  • *desert the church* – verse 19
  • *deny the Christ* – verses 22-23.
  • *deceive the Christian* – verse 26

The devil is out to get you. How can we counteract the spirit of antichrist that is so prevalent? Well, we need to stay in the church of God (verse 19); we need to feed on the Word of God (verse 24) and we need to rely on the Spirit of God (verse 27).

In Chapter 2 verses 28 and 29, there is the *Barrier of Sinfulness.*

How do you want to meet the Lord? Is Christ going to catch you red-handed with things in your life you do not want to be there when He appears? Would it not be awful for the Lord to come and find you displaying your old nature? Would it not be terrible for Christ to come and find you at loggerheads with your brother or sister in Christ? When Christ appears, what way will you meet Him?

God is light, God is holy - and the Bible reminds us: *"Follow peace with all men, and holiness, without which no man shall see the Lord"* (Hebrews 12:14).

(2) GOD IS LOVE
Chapter 3 - Chapter 4

Do you see what John says in Chapter 4 verse 16?

"And we have known and believed the love that God hath to us. God is love; and he that dwelleth in love dwelleth in God, and God in him."

Love is part of the very being and nature of God. If we are united to God through faith in Christ, we share His nature.

Remember that Christian love means that we treat each other the way God treats us.

Most of us interpret love as a feeling. We think of love as an emotional thing. But love is an act of the will. I must choose to treat you the way God treats me. Tragically and sadly, this kind of love is often missing among believers.

The words: *"love"* and *"loveth"* occur 43 times in this letter. They cover many aspects of the Christian life, such as: *"Why we love God"* (1 John 4:19); *"We should love one another"* (1 John 4:7) and *"How this love may be developed"* (1 John 2:5).

John tell us that we need to be marked by:

(a) PURE LOVE
Chapter 3 verses 1-10

Righteous love!

How many times have you been told that salvation is in three tenses?

We *have been* saved from the penalty of sin.
We *are being* saved from the power of sin.
Someday, we *will be* saved from the presence of sin.

The problem is that too many of us are still too tense about the second tense.

We hear that we are being saved from the power of sin, but for many of us, if that statement is true, then our salvation has not yet taken full effect!

Do you want to have: *"Victory in Jesus"* and not just sing about it?

How?

Through the work of the Saviour.

Why did He die? He died to make you holy.

"And ye know that He was manifested to take away our sins; and in Him is no sin" (1 John 3:5).

How?

Through the walk of the saint.

Here we have some of John's uncompromising statements about sin.

"Whosoever abideth in Him sinneth not" (1 John 3:6).

"He that committeth sin is of the devil" (1 John 3:8).

"Whosoever is born of God doth not commit sin" (1 John 3:9).

We are not sinless, we never will be this side of Heaven, but are we sinning less and less as time marches on?

Victory in Jesus. How?

Through the witness of the Spirit.

Is this not another reason why Christians cannot practise sin? It is incompatible with the ministry of the Holy Spirit who has imparted a new nature to us (2 Peter 1:4).

That is why this love is to be pure love.

(b) PRACTICAL LOVE
Chapter 3 verses 11-24

If you want to know the true meaning of love, you will not find it in the dictionary, you will not find it in a romantic novel, you will not find it in a soap opera. You will only find it at the Cross of Christ.

John says:

"Hereby perceive we the love of God, because He laid down His life for us: and we ought to lay down our lives for the brethren" (1 John 3:16).

John is saying:

"If Christ loved you enough to die for you, you ought to love your brother enough to live for him."

You see, Christian love is personal, active and practical.

We talk about helping that *"brother or sister in need"* and we talk and talk, but what good does it do, if we never do anything about it?

We talk about soul-winning and bringing people to hear the gospel and we talk and talk, but what good does it do if we never do anything about it?

Talk is cheap, but this love is practical.

(c) PERCEIVING LOVE
Chapter 4 verses 1-6

It is a love that perceives truth and error. Look at Chapter 4 verse 3:

"And every spirit that confesseth not that Jesus Christ is come in the flesh is not of God: and this is that spirit of antichrist, whereof ye have heard that it should come; and even now already is it in the world."

Or, we could translate it like this:

"Every spirit that confesseth not that Jesus is Christ come in the flesh is not of God."

"Jesus" is the name of the Saviour's humanity. *"Christ"* is the title of His deity.

Do you see what John is saying? He is saying that any teacher who does not confess the full deity and the full humanity of Christ is to be identified among the antichrists (1 John 2:18). The crucial question is always this: *"What think ye of Christ? whose son is He?"* (Matthew 22:42). What people think about Jesus Christ is the touchstone of correctness in matters of the faith. How can you tell a faithful preacher of the Word? They will be one hundred percent clear on the person and work of Jesus Christ. Check them out. That is why you ought to bring your Bible. Check me out!

(d) PERFECT LOVE
Chapter 4 verses 7-21

Do you see what John says in Chapter 4 verse 18?

"There is no fear in love; but perfect love casteth out fear: because fear hath torment. He that feareth is not made perfect in love."

The emphasis is on perfect love, love that has reached maturity, love that is complete.

Do you want to stand before the Lord and be able to look Him in the eye?

Well, let me ask you, do you love your brother or sister in Christ? John says that if you claim to love the Lord and yet at the same time detest your brother, you are a liar. Is this what God is calling you? A liar.

How can you claim to love the invisible when you do not love the visible?

How can you claim to love the Lord and not love His people?

(3) GOD IS LIFE
Chapter 5

Do you see what John says in Chapter 5 verse 11?

"This is the record, that God hath given to us eternal life, and this life is in His Son."

We notice here:

(a) THE ACCEPTANCE OF THIS LIFE
Chapter 5 verses 1-5

This new life begins with a new birth. *"Whosoever believeth that Jesus is the Christ is born of God"* (1 John 5:1). When John uses the word *"believe"* he actually means what we mean by the word *"receive"*. This statement is explained by John 1 verse 12: *"But as many as received Him."*

Have you received Him? Are you saved? Of course, one of the marks of this new life is a desire to obey God. Another mark is that you will want to have victory over the world.

(b) THE ASSURANCE OF THIS LIFE
Chapter 5 verses 6-13

> *'Tis a point I long to know,*
> *Oft it causes anxious thought;*
> *Do I love the Lord, or no?*
> *Am I His, or am I not?*
> (John Newton)

Is this not one of the reasons why John wrote this letter?

Look at verse 13:

"These things have I written unto you that believe on the name of the Son of God; that ye may know that ye have eternal life, and that ye may believe on the name of the Son of God."

Some say: *"Well, you cannot really know that you are going to heaven!"*

Yet John says: *"You can!"*

How? How can we know for sure?

Well, His Work for me makes me Sure

We are saved by Jesus Christ who, we are told in verse 6, *"came by water and blood"*.

Do you recall what these false teachers were saying? They were saying that the Lord Jesus was a human being and that the divine Christ came upon Him at His baptism and departed before His crucifixion.

This would mean we have no Saviour at all. No! says John. Here are two witnesses to prove that Jesus Christ is God. He was declared to be the Son of God at His baptism (Matthew 3:17). He was proved to be the Son of God at His death (John 8:28 and Chapter 12:28-33). On both occasions, at His baptism (*"by water"*) and on the Cross (*"and blood"*), the Father testified to the deity of His Son.

His Witness in me makes me Sure

The witness of the Holy Spirit is reliable. John says: *"the Spirit is truth"* (verse 6).

Now how do I know that Jesus Christ is my Saviour and Lord? Well, look at verse 10:

"He that believeth on the Son of God hath the witness in himself."

The moment we believe on the Lord Jesus, the Holy Spirit enters our hearts to abide there forever and *"the Spirit ... beareth witness with our spirit, that we are the children of God"* (Romans 8:16).

But there is something else here:

His Word to me makes me Sure

"These things have I have written unto you" (verse 13). This refers to the Scripture, the Word of God. Christian assurance is simply a matter of taking God at His Word.

But notice:

(c) THE ACTIVITY OF THIS LIFE
   Chapter 5 verses 14-21

This new life we have in Christ will be active in *prayer* (verses 13-17); in *holiness* (verse 18) and in *knowledge* (verses 19-21).

Do you see again John's repeated use of the word: *"know"*?

"We know that the Son of God is come" (verse 20). The heretics knew nothing!

"We may know Him that is true."

John cannot seem to say it enough:

"The Lord Jesus is the Son of God. The Man of Calvary is God's Son, Jesus Christ."

Do you see here that John sets forth the **Humanity of Christ?** *"The Son of God is come."*
Do you see here that John sets forth the **Deity of Christ?** *"This is the true God, and eternal life"* (verse 20).

Then John gives one last word of warning:

"Little children, keep yourselves from idols" (verse 21).

What has that got to do with what John has talked about?

Do you recall the description of John's letter as being like a spiraling staircase? Well, we have climbed all the way to the top of the staircase and what do we find? It is the throne room of deity. Who is there?

It is Jesus Christ as God, and John tells us that anything that is short of Jesus Christ revealed as God is idolatry.

Are you guilty of theological idolatry? Have you a sub-standard view of Christ? Maybe your idol is not mental, it is monetary, it is material. Of course, an idol is any substitute for God. Your house, your car, your children, your home, your job, your clothes, anything that comes between you and your Lord. Whatever it is, have you enthroned it in your heart? Is it taking the place of God and *"His Son Jesus Christ"*?

Is it time for you to pray with William Cowper?

> *"The dearest idol I have known,*
> *Whate'er that idol be*
> *Help me to tear it from Thy throne,*
> *And worship only Thee."*

CHAPTER 24

2 John

Most ladies agree that the best presents come in small packages!

Also, some of the choicest pieces of literature could be written on a postcard! The 2nd epistle of John has often been referred to as *"a postcard"* for it is short enough to fit on a single sheet of papyrus.

It is one of five single chapter books in the Bible. We have the prophet Obadiah in the Old Testament and Philemon, 2 John, 3 John and Jude in the New Testament. *These books have often been described as God's special post-it notes to His people.* They are short yet significant. They are brief yet beneficial.

2 John may be the most neglected book in the New Testament. I can never recall hearing a message preached from this book. Have you? Yet the Lord used the apostle John to write about the essentials of the Christian life.

When we come to this postcard of 2 John, there are several matters we need to keep in mind:

1. There is the Question of Identity

Who wrote this little letter and to whom did he write it?

Almost all scholars agree that the human author of this postcard epistle is John. This book was freely quoted by the early church writers. Also, the language and style would confirm that it was written by John who wrote the Gospel and the first epistle of John. Lamoyne Sharpe makes the point: *"This epistle very closely resembles*

John's first epistle and eight out of the thirteen verses of this epistle are in substance found in the first."

But to whom did John write? Who is the *"elect lady and her children"*?

Some have supposed that *"the elect lady"* was a figurative term to denote the Christian church in general. Others have suggested that it was sent to a particular but unnamed church. But, if that were so, John would have clearly stated it in his epistle.

Is it not better to understand this phrase in a normal plain sense? Referring to a particular woman and her children rather than interpreting it in a non-literal sense as a church and its membership? This would mean that the last verse of the letter: *"The children of thy elect sister greet thee"* (verse 13) would mean the nephews or nieces of the person addressed in verse 1.

Now it is accurate to say that John does address a group in this letter, for we find the *plural tense* used in verses 6, 8, 10 and 12, but it is also true that he addresses an individual as is clear from verses 1, 4, 5 and 13.

Maybe the solution is that a Christian assembly was meeting in this home, along with the family of *"the elect lady"* so that John had both the family and the congregation in mind. Were there not similar situations in other places? Do you recall Paul's recurring phrase? *"The church in thy house"* (Romans 16:5, 1 Corinthians 16:19, Colossians 4:15 and Philemon 2).

So here is John addressing a Christian lady and her children and the church which met in her house.

2. There is the Question of Orthodoxy

2 John deals with the same problem as 1 John. False teachers began to arise, infecting the church with false doctrine. This teaching eventually became known as Gnosticism.

Dr. Andrew Telford (1895-1997) said:

*"False teachers were going from place to place trying to gain an audience.
They Denied that Jesus Christ had come in the flesh.
They Deviated from the teachings of Christ.
They Deceived new converts to their own advantage.
They came preaching another so-called gospel. They presented a different
Christ from the One John's converts knew."*

These Gnostics claimed to have superior knowledge but they denied the basic teaching about the incarnation and the humanity of our Lord Jesus Christ. They attacked the person of Christ - and He is the touchstone of truth. The person and work of Jesus Christ are of crucial importance.

John's purpose was to strengthen Christians to resist the tide of heresy that was rising against the church.

3. There is the Question of Hospitality

When this letter was written, there was no complete Bible. This necessitated a special ministry of prophets and teachers who imparted and interpreted New Testament truth to the church. These travelling preachers were highly esteemed and quickly attained a leading role in the community. Such men would travel from place to place in a much needed teaching ministry. They were travelling preachers who would spend a few days here and then move on to somewhere else. The problem was, where would they stay? In those days, the inns were immoral, dirty and flea-infested. So what were the circuit riding preachers supposed to do?

What else could they do, but stay with the believers who would provide them with a good square meal and a clean bed?

But what was happening here was this: among these preachers were false teachers.

As John MacArthur says:

"They seemed to be conducting an itinerant ministry among John's

congregations, seeking to make converts, and taking advantage of Christian hospitality to advance their cause."

Lucian writes about an itinerant charlatan who lived off the generosity of Christians. As soon as he was found out, he moved to another company of equally benevolent guileless believers.

"The Didache", an early Christian document, lays down regulations about hospitality to travelling preachers. It states:

"If he that comes is a passer-by, succour him as far as you can, but he shall not stay with you longer than two or three days, unless there be a necessity. But if he is minded to settle among you and be a craftsman, let him work and eat. But if he has no trade according to your understanding, provide that he shall not live idle among you, being a Christian. But if he will not do this, he is a Christmonger, a trafficker in Christ, of such men beware."

Was it the case that the front door of *"the elect lady"* was always open? Did she not have the heart to say: *"No!"* to anyone?

Could it have been that she had shown hospitality to these false prophets?

Or was it that John feared that these false teachers would take advantage of her kindness?

Whatever the situation was, John writes this letter to warn his readers against showing hospitality to such deceivers (verse 10).

His message is:

"Make sure your love is discerning. Hospitality and kindness must be given only to those who are adhering to the fundamentals of the faith."

Is John's letter relevant? Well, we live in a day of ecumenical evangelism when people demand that we accept and support the union of believers and apostates. Surely in such a day we need to remember John's teaching. The Bible says: *"Be ye not unequally yoked together with unbelievers"* (2 Corinthians 6:14).

Doctrine matters! What we believe concerning the person and work of Christ matters. It is truth that determines the bounds of love and, as a consequence, the bounds of unity.

Now in order to open up this letter, I want to underscore three words in the opening verse: *"The elect lady"*.

"The elect lady":

(1) IS CONSIDERED BY THE APOSTLE
verses 1-3

He writes this letter to her. Now this is:

(a) A PERSONAL LETTER

1. Look at Him

"The elder unto the elect lady"

"The elder" - that is a term which comes from the Greek word: *"presbyteros"* and it has the general meaning of: *"an old man"*.

So, it could refer here to *Maturity*: not necessarily indicating old age, but rather indicating someone who was the last survivor of those who had seen the Lord. John's knowledge of the gospel went back a lot further than his present contemporaries.

Of course, the word could refer to *Ministry*: for this was a word given to a particular class who had the care of the churches. Peter went down a similar line when he described himself as a fellow elder (1 Peter 5:1). So here we see John the apostle referring to himself as an elder.

Reliable sources tell us that in the latter days of his life, before he went home to be with the Lord, John was ministering to the flock at Ephesus. Of course, in the local church today there are elders appointed by the Holy Spirit (Acts 20:28). God gives gifts sovereignly, uniquely and personally. These elders are to act as shepherds who feed and lead the flock (Hebrews 13:7, 17).

The elders have a responsibility to the church.
The church has a responsibility to the elders.

2. Look at Her

"The elect lady." It can be translated: *"the elect Kyria"* or: *"the elect Electa".* One scholar has tried to identify this lady and suggests that as the Greek *" Kyria,"* is the Hebrew *"Martha",* she could have been *"Martha of Bethany".* This is hardly likely as this letter was addressed to the *"elect lady and her children"* and, as far as we know, Martha, Mary and Lazarus never married.

I believe that John is writing to a godly mother, someone who is a devoted follower of the Lord Jesus Christ, someone who has had the joy of seeing some of her children come to saving faith in Christ.

Here was a lady who was following in the footsteps of Philemon and many others when she made her home available for the various meetings of the Assembly (Philemon 2).

If this is true, then 2 John is the only book in the Bible that is addressed to a woman and it is a commendation of a Christian mother.

So this is a personal letter from John to a godly mother whom John was deeply concerned about.

Can you see in the opening remarks John's restraint?

As John Phillips points out:

"John uses the term 'beloved' when writing to a church or to a man but he uses no such familiarity in addressing a woman, not even when writing to a sister in Christ."

We need to be careful in our relationships with the opposite sex.

(b) A DOCTRINAL LETTER

Do you notice that in the first 4 verses of this letter John uses the word *"truth"* five times? He also uses the word *"love"* four times in these opening verses.

When you put those two words together, you can see the emphasis that John intended in this short letter. He was saying:

"I want you to understand what Christian love is. It is walking in truth."

How important it is not to separate those two things.
To practise truth without love leads to legalism.
To practise love without truth leads to liberalism.

Truth and love!

These two qualities ought to mark our lives as Christians.

Someone once said that a well-balanced Christian life contains salt and sugar. Salt is truth and sugar is love. Some Christians want only the salt. They are all truth without love. They can be cold and judgmental, having no concern for the feelings, needs or hurts of others. Others are only sugar bowls. They are all love and no truth. They do not want to be held accountable. They do not want to be confronted with sin. All they want is for you to be nice to them. All they want is sugar.

Our goal as believers is to keep truth and love, salt and sugar in balance. Is this not how our Lord lived? Did He not walk in truth and love? (John 8:7-11). Paul combines the two when he says: *"but speaking the truth in love"* (Ephesians 4:15).

Here heresy was making inroads into the church, so John writes this doctrinal letter where:

1. Truth is EMPHASISED

David Jackman says:

"The truth of God revealed supremely in the living Word and recorded

unerringly in the written Word provides the route by which the Christian is travelling from earth to heaven."

The *"truth"* is the whole body of Christian teaching, later called by John: *"the doctrine of Christ"* (verse 9). The Bible, the Word of God, is the truth of God (John 17:17). John opened this letter on this note of *"truth"* because there were false teachers abroad who were spreading error (verse 7). John was not one to say that all teaching is true in one way or another and that we should not be critical as long as folk are sincere. *No!* To John there was a great difference, in fact a deadly difference between truth and error - and he would not tolerate error.

All we hear about today in our ecumenical climate is: *love*. We have been told to set aside doctrinal differences and the things to which we hold tenaciously and just love one another. Now, we certainly ought *"to love one another"* (verse 5). Is there not far too much bickering, strife, and discord among believers? But, it is *never correct to lay aside doctrine for love*. Christian love operates in the sphere of truth.

2. Truth is EXPERIENCED

In verse 2, John writes:

"For the truth's sake, which dwelleth in us, and shall be with us for ever."

The *"truth"* is not only an objective revelation but a subjective experience in our lives. We can know the truth!

How did this elect lady and her children come to know the truth and become children of God? Through the *"grace and mercy of God"* (verse 3). You see, when you receive grace and mercy from God, you then experience His *peace*.

3. Truth is EMBODIED

"Grace be with you, mercy, and peace, from God the Father, and from the Lord Jesus Christ, the Son of the Father, in truth and love" (verse 3).

Jesus Christ is the truth (John 14:6). Here John declares His Deity. He is: *"the Son of the Father"*.

It has been well said that it is possible to discover where a person stands by where he is prepared to place Jesus Christ.

You see, the Christian faith stands or falls on the doctrine of the Deity of Jesus Christ.

If He is only man, then He cannot save us. If He is not God come in flesh, then the Christian faith is lies not truth - and John opened his letter with the wrong emphasis.

Some years ago, the great American statesman Daniel Webster was dining in Boston with a group of distinguished men, some of whom had Unitarian leanings. The Unitarians deny the Trinity and also the Deity of both the Son and the Spirit. When the subject of religion came up, Webster affirmed his belief in the deity of Jesus Christ and his confidence in the work of atonement.

"But Mr. Webster", said one man, *"Can you comprehend how Christ can be both God and man?"*

"No, Sir, I cannot comprehend it", Webster replied.

"If I could comprehend Him, He would be no greater than myself, and I feel that I need a superhuman Saviour."

Do you realise that the person of Christ is the fundamental test of Christian doctrine? The question that should be continually upon our lips is this: *"What think ye of Christ?"*

Truth is embodied in a person and that person is Jesus Christ.

4. Truth is EXPRESSED

How can you express truth? By walking in it! By regulating your life according to the truth. By living in the light of the truth.

J. B. Hewitt sums it up beautifully when he says:

"Truth is in the Christian Intellectually. In his mind, he holds the truth.

Truth is in the Christian Sympathetically. In his heart, he loves the truth.

Truth is in the Christian Authoritatively. In his soul, he lives the truth."

So **the elect lady** is considered by the apostle. And also:

(2) IS COMMENDED BY THE APOSTLE
verse 4

Look at verse 4:

"I rejoiced greatly that I found of thy children walking in truth, as we have received a commandment from the Father."

Keep in mind that John is addressing this lady and her family and possibly the church that met in her home. They were living in a society that was absolutely pagan and godless. Think of:

(a) THE TRUTH THAT WAS TAUGHT IN THIS HOME

Here was a woman who had taught her children the truth and they were maturing in the things of God.

Now the literal translation of verse 4 is: *"some of thy children"*. Did that indicate that there were others who had gone their own way and done their own thing? Was this family just like many more? The truth had been taught, yet they had not experienced household salvation.

What does God expect in a Christian home?

What does God expect from a Christian home?

Do you notice that this family were *well-balanced?* They had truth and love.

They were *well-behaved.* They were walking in the truth of God.

They were *well-blessed.* They were loved by all the believers who entered their home.

Is my home different from the home of unbelievers next door?
Is my home a place where God is honoured?
Is it a home where His Word is revered, read and expounded?
Is it a home where His people are welcomed?
What about our children?
Do we seek to: *"bring them up in the nuture and admonition of the Lord"* (Ephesians 6:4)?
Do you pray with them and for them?
Do you teach them the Word of God?
Do you bring them out to hear the Word of God?

Here is a Christian mother who had the unsurpassed joy of seeing at least some of her children walk in her footsteps.

Susannah Wesley had seventeen children – John and Charles and fifteen others - yet she made time to be alone with God for one hour every day to plead for their salvation.

(b) THE JOY THAT WAS BROUGHT TO THIS HEART

As John sees this family living for the Lord, he is refreshed and encouraged. To *"walk in the truth"* means to obey it, to permit it to control every area of our lives. It is possible that John had led this lady and some of her children to Christ. John's joy was that the elect lady's children were walking in truth.

It certainly brings joy to the Father when He sees His children obeying His Word.

We who are in spiritual leadership also have great joy when we see believers walking in the truth - submitting to the Word of God, obeying the Lord in Believer's Baptism and meeting to remember the Lord Jesus in the Lord's Supper.

When the great Baptist preacher, Charles Spurgeon, was a lad, he lived with his grandfather who pastored a church in Stambourne, England. A church member named Roads used to sit in the local pub and drink beer and smoke. This practice grieved the pastor very much. One day, Charles said to his grandfather: *"I'll kill old Roads, I will."*

He went to the pub. He confronted Roads in the pub with these words:

"What doest thou here, Elijah? Sitting with the ungodly, and you a member of a church and breaking your pastor's heart. I'm ashamed of you. I wouldn't break my pastor's heart, I'm sure."

Do you know what happened? It was not long before Roads showed up at the pastor's home, confessing his sins and apologising for his behaviour. Young Spurgeon had *"killed him"* indeed!

Would John, if he knew you, rejoice over you and commend you? Do you bring joy to the hearts of your spiritual leaders? Are they refreshed and encouraged when they look at you? Do they see you walking in truth?

Then **the elect lady**:

(3) IS COMMANDED BY THE APOSTLE
verses 5-6

John wanted the elect lady and her family and the church meeting in her home to: *"love one another"*. Now notice:

(a) THE WHERE OF THIS COMMAND

Where did this command initiate? In the Upper Room! In John 13.

If you read the Upper Room ministry in John 13 to 17, this word *"love"* occurs some 26 times. Whatever else the Lord Jesus intended to impress upon the disciples, He wanted this to live with them and live in them. He says:

"A new commandment I give unto you, That ye love one another, as I have loved you, that ye also love one another. By this shall all men know that ye are My disciples, if ye have love one to another" (John 13:34-35).

Here is the badge, the identifying mark of the true believer: if you have love one to another. The Lord Jesus could see down through the ages. He knew that His people would be living in a hostile environment that they would experience trial and hardship, and so He says: *"Do not hate one another. Do not be unkind. Do not be discourteous. Love one another."*

What have you done with the Lord's command? Has brotherly love *"gone out through the window"*? Are you marked by love or have you allowed jealousy and bitterness to well up within your heart?

(b) THE WHO OF THIS COMMAND

Who did this command include? John says: *"one another"*.

I heard about a prestigious Baptist church in the U.S.A. who were appointing a new assistant pastor. There was a great disagreement over who it should be. The discussions were lively, but eventually one man was chosen and he was appointed. The day came for the induction service and it was televised. There was great excitement. This had never happened before. After the hymns, the pastor elect stood to his feet, but one of his greatest opponents could not take it anymore. He strode up to the front to the podium, planted an upper cut on his chin in front of the congregation and the whole audience that was watching on television.

What do you think that communicated to the outside world? What did it say about the Lord's words: *"By this shall all men know that ye are My disciples, if ye have love one to another"* (John 13:35)?

The young pastor did not retaliate and that attitude made all the difference. That young pastor was a man called Charles Stanley,who has become one of the greatest Bible teachers in America. It was his attitude that made the difference.

I wonder what the community really thinks of your local church. Do they say: *"See how these Christians love one another!"*?

(c) THE WHAT OF THIS COMMAND

What did this command involve?

Well, the world tells us: *"love is a many-splendored thing"* and *"love is all we need"*, but John defines love like this in verse 6:

"And this is love, that we walk after His commandments. This is the commandment, That, as ye have heard from the beginning, ye should walk in it."

In verse 5, obedience finds expression in love.
In verse 6, love finds expression in obedience.

Children love their parents by obeying them. Love is obeying the Lord. He says: *"If ye love Me, keep My commandments"* (John 14:15). Walking in love means we walk in obedience to the Word of God. Christian love is an act of the will. It simply means treating each other the way God treats us.

God forgives us, so we forgive one another.
God receives us, so we receive one another.
God is kind to us, so we are kind to one another.

How tragic it is when Christians claim to love the Bible and hate the brethren.

Where there is a sincere love for the Word of God, there will be a sincere love for the people of God.

"Love never faileth,
Love is pure gold,
Love is what Jesus
Came to unfold."

The elect lady:

(4) IS CAUTIONED BY THE APOSTLE
verses 7-13

The Canon of Scripture was not complete. Itinerant ministry was the order of the day. Hospitality was being shown to the servants of God, but there were those who took advantage of it. Wandering, vagabond preachers were popping up everywhere, expounding all sorts of doctrine that was striking at the very roots of Christianity.

Though this *"elect lady"* was a stalwart for the truth, John still felt the need to warn her and all like her, especially women, to be on their guard.

So he warns here about:

(a) THOSE THAT DECEIVE

"For many deceivers are entered into the world, who confess not that Jesus Christ is come in the flesh. This is a deceiver and an antichrist" (verse 7).

John is talking about those false teachers, mentioned in his first letter, who did not believe in the incarnation, the literal coming into human existence of the Lord Jesus.

Where did these false teachers come from originally? John says: *"for many deceivers have gone out into the world"*. It seems likely that they had gone out from the church. At one time, they professed to believe *"the faith which was once delivered unto the saints"* (Jude verse 3), but they turned from that faith and abandoned the truth and the church.

John says in his first epistle: *"They went out from us, but they were not of us"* (1 John 2:19).

Do you recall Paul's warning to the Ephesian elders?

"For I know this, that after my departure shall grievous wolves enter in among you, not sparing the flock. Also of your own selves shall men arise, speaking perverse things, to draw away disciples after them" (Acts 20:29-30).

Mark those words: *"of your own selves"*. Did you know that the founders of many cults came out of orthodox evangelical Christianity? Does the name William Irvine ring a bell? He professed faith in Christ in 1895, joined the Faith Mission in 1896 becoming a strong leader and dynamic preacher. Then, all of a sudden, Irvine changed tact and began denouncing the churches. He set himself as up as a special leader and teacher and gathered a group of people around him to be known later as: The Cooneyites. They preach: *"the Jesus way"* and teach that salvation is through imitating the life of Christ.

Eventually, in 1920, Irvine went to live in Jerusalem, for he believed that he was one of the two witnesses mentioned in Revelation 11. In 1947, he died. Three and a half days later, he did not rise again like the two witnesses will. Still he lies in the grave, testimony to the fact that he was a false prophet who spawned a false cult.

Do you see what John is saying?

If you err concerning the person of Christ, it is proof that you are not a child of God.

John describes these teachers as antichrist because they deny that He is indeed God come in the flesh. They gave their converts a substitute Christ who is not the Christ of the New Testament.

You see, the first question you want to ask any teacher, preacher, author is: *"What do you think of Christ? Is He God come in the flesh?"*

If he hesitates or if he denies that Jesus is God come in the flesh, then you can be sure you have a false teacher.

(b) THOSE THAT DESTROY

John says:
"Look to yourselves, that we lose not those things which we have wrought, but that we receive a full reward" (verse 8).

"Look to yourselves!" Beware! Take heed!

A believer cannot lose his salvation but he can certainly lose his testimony and he can lose his reward, and it is a serious thing to be led astray by someone's false doctrine.

What a tragedy it is when God's servants labour faithfully to build up a work and then the work is destroyed by false teaching (Galatians 4:11 and 2 Peter 1:10).

Do we not need to discriminate fellowship on the basis of adherence to the truth? (Colossians 2:18-19 and Chapter 3:24-25)

(c) THOSE THAT DEPART

"Whosoever transgresseth, and abideth not in the doctrine of Christ, hath not God. He that abideth in the doctrine of Christ, he hath both the Father and the Son" (verse 9).

The word *"trangresseth"* means: *"to run ahead too far, to pass beyond the assigned limits"* or *"to go onward"*. It is a dig at those who claimed to have advanced knowledge. The reference is to people who go beyond the doctrine of Christ. This is characteristic of every false cult. They have some new information, some new book, some new revelation by some new prophet.

Do you see how cut and dried John is?

"Either you hold to the historic doctrines of the Christian faith or you do not.

If you do, you are a genuine believer, united to the Father and the Son. If you do not, you are deceived and have not God."

Truth then, boils down to doctrine.

Truth always comes down to doctrine.
It was so in John's day.

It was so in Martin Luther's day when he stood before all the massed might of Rome.

It is so in our day. We are inundated with cults that attack all the great fundamentals of the faith and who decry doctrine claiming it to be divisive and an obstacle to their vision of a global, ecumenical church.

No wonder John says: *"Watch, take heed, beware!"*

They may be gifted and charming, may drop the names of believers into the conversation, may say many true things. But out it will come, some subtle serious error, concerning the person of Christ, the ministry of the Holy Spirit or the inerrancy and inspiration of Scripture.

(d) THOSE THAT DISCIPLE

Verse 10 is a powerful statement:

"If there come any unto you, and bring not this doctrine, receive him not into your house, neither bid him God speed."

What doctrine? The doctrine of the Deity of Christ.

You may think: *"Oh, that is so harsh! That is so unloving! Brother John, you don't love people!"*

Well, although John was called *"the apostle of love"*, he was also the standard bearer of truth. An old story describes how strong he was. While he was living in Ephesus, one day he went to the public baths. A false teacher named Cerinthus arrived. Cerinthus taught that the Lord Jesus was the natural son of Joseph and Mary, not God come in the flesh. He said that the divine Christ came upon Christ at His baptism and left Him before His crucifixion. John jumped out of the water, got his clothes and towel, and took off running.

He said:
"Let us hurry from this house, lest it fall on us. Cerinthus, the enemy of truth, is here."

We must not allow the ***poison of false doctrine to get into our home.***

If the Jehovah's Witnesses or the Mormons call at your home, do not bring them in. We do not have to be rude or impolite about it, but John says, *"Do not welcome the cultist when he comes and do not greet him when he goes, for if you do you may be an accomplice in a wicked work which may send souls to their eternal ruin".*

We must not allow ***the poison of false doctrine to get into our church.***

In an age when experience takes precedence over truth, may we *"prove all things, hold fast that which is good"* (1 Thessalonians 5:21).

CHAPTER 25

3 John

How many times have you struggled in a local church situation and said to yourself:

"If only we could be committed like the First Century church"?

We read the New Testament and get the impression that the early church was like the Garden of Eden - perfect. However, as we journey back in time, the *"travel brochures"* of the New Testament depict quite a different setting. There was the scorching heat of persecution, accompanied by the flies and ants of heresy that needed constant swatting. Then, like sand in your bathing suit, there were always abrasive people in the church who got under your skin and rubbed you up the wrong way. It was not the Garden of Eden that we like to imagine.

When we turn to this picture postcard of 3 John, the shortest New Testament epistle in the original Greek, John captures for us one of the most vivid pictures of the New Testament church in the First Century.

Here we have a golden opportunity to be a fly on the wall and eavesdrop on all that is happening. We even encounter a smattering of early church politics!

This letter was written to an individual believer. He was possibly one of the leaders but certainly one of the members of a local church.

3 John is perhaps the most personal of John's three epistles. 1 John appears to be a general letter addressed to churches throughout

Asia Minor; 2 John was sent to a lady and her family, but in 3 John the apostle clearly names the only recipient as: *"the wellbeloved Gaius"*. The name *"Gaius"* means *"earthy"*.

These last two letters by John are very moving. The aged apostle in his first letter was concerned about the inroads of apostasy. He then adds a postscript in his second letter, then another in his third letter. Taking the three letters together they are very brief. In the first letter, there are about 2,350 words; in the second only 245 words, and although 2 John may be the shortest epistle as far as the number of verses is concerned, 3 John has fewer words. In fact, only 219 words in total.

I wonder, does John sense the desperate urgency of the situation? He is the last of the apostles. He is an old man, living in Ephesus. He puts down his pen, picks it up again, then puts it down, picks it up again and puts it down a third time.

The times, like ours, are uncertain. Persecution, error, apostasy, and Christians squabbling - so John writes and writes and writes. Both 2 and 3 John are the shortest epistles in the New Testament. They could fit on a single papyrus sheet (verse 13). But, do not underestimate their importance because of their brevity.

As John Phillips says:

"It is a mistake to measure the man by the size of his manuscript - the Holy Spirit does not always inspire long books to convey vital beliefs."

As we come to consider this book, there are some things I want you to notice by way of introduction.

1. SIMILARITIES

In many ways, both 2 John and 3 John bear a striking resemblance.

For example:
They are almost the same length.
They were probably written at the same time around 90-95 A.D. in

the city of Ephesus in the latter part of John's life.

They both give us a glimpse into the life of the early church near the end of the First Century.

They both address the very important issue of hospitality and the church's attitude to itinerant preachers.

2. CONTRASTS

2 John was written to a lady and her children: 3 John was written to a man and his acquaintances.

The first is about somebody who was *"too soft"*: the second is about somebody who was *"too hard"*.

In one, there is an example of hospitality which is forbidden: in the other, there is an example of hospitality which is encouraged.

In his second letter, John is saying: *"The truth is worth standing for"*: in his third letter, he is saying: *"The truth is worth working for"*.

In the second letter, no personal names are mentioned: in this third letter, 3 specific names are mentioned, namely Gaius, Diotrephes, and Demetrius.

3. PERSONALITIES

The main divisions of this book centre around three characters:

Gaius, to whom the letter is written, a Christian of grace and generosity.

Diotrephes, a problem personality, a pain in the neck, and sadly someone who is still with us today!

Demetrius, a trustworthy and truthful Christian.

These three have been described in different ways.

David Jackman speaks about:

Gaius a Christian Friend.
Diotrephes a Christian Fraud.
Demetrius a Christian Follower.

J. B. Hewitt talks about:

Gaius as a Beloved Brother.
Diotrephes as a Bigoted Brother.
Demetrius as Balanced Brother.

Warren Wiersbe sees the three men like this:

Gaius as a Prosperous Christian.
Diotrephes as a Proud Christian.
Demetrius as a Pleasant Christian.

Raymond Brown says that:

Gaius Serves Others.
Diotrephes Hinders Others.
Demetrius Attracts Others.

Now, I want you to see that:

(1) In *GAIUS*, we have a picture of CHARITY

The word *"charity"* (*"agape"*) in verse 6 - *"borne witness of thy charity before the church"* - should be translated *"love"* since it is the particular word used for divine love. Here was a man who loved the Lord (verse 2); loved the Word of God (verse 3) and loved the people of God (verse 5).

In the New Testament, we find a number of men with this name, Gaius. Like *"Jim"* or *"John"* in our day, Gaius was a common name in the Roman world. Indeed we meet this name several times in the New Testament.

There was a *Gaius of Corinth* (Romans 16:23 and 1 Corinthians 1:14) who was Paul's host when he was in that city. It would seem that he was one of the very few people that Paul had personally baptised.

Then there was *Gaius of Macedonia* who accompanied Paul and who was present at the riot in Ephesus (Acts 19:29).

There was *Gaius of Derbe* who was Paul's travelling companion and who accompanied him to Jerusalem with the collection for the poor saints (Acts 20:4).

We have no way of knowing if the Gaius addressed by John was one of these. However, he was a man much loved by the aged apostle (verses 1 and 5). Indeed, if Gaius were a member of our church, we would not have any trouble loving him either. You see, John talks here about some qualities that marked him out. He refers to:

(a) HIS PHYSICAL DEBILITY
Verses 1-2

"The elder unto the wellbeloved Gaius, whom I love in the truth. Beloved, I wish above all things that thou mayest prosper and be in health, even as thy soul prospereth."

It seems that Gaius was unwell. Could it have been that his energy was spent because of his selfless ministry to the servants of God? Whatever the explanation, he was physically weak.

Incidentally, this is one of the verses that is used to teach: *"the prosperity gospel, the health and wealth gospel"*. A gospel that promises health and wealth to those who respond to the message. When the promises fail to materialise and followers get sick or lose their jobs, they are told that either they do not have faith or else there is sin in their lives.

Surely the example of Gaius actually contradicts this? Here was a man whose spiritual condition was exemplary, while his physical condition was poor. Did Gaius not have enough faith? Was there sin in his life? *Not at all.* Never assume that because a believer is unwell that there is sin in his life. That may indeed be the explanation (1 Corinthians 11:30), but we cannot make that assumption.

Notice also that John prays that Gaius might be well. It is important to take care of our bodies. Do you recall Paul's words to the young Timothy? *"For bodily exercise profiteth little"* (1 Timothy 4:8).
Have you discovered that the physical and the spiritual are closely related?

(b) HIS SPIRITUAL PROSPERITY
Verse 2

His soul was prospering.

Do you recall that in the Old Testament a person's spiritual prosperity could be measured by their material prosperity? The Old Testament blessing was: *"The blessing of the LORD, it maketh rich, and He addeth no sorrow with it"* (Proverbs 10:22).

> Job was rich (Job 1:3).
> Abraham was rich (Genesis 13:2).
> Jacob was rich (Genesis 30:43).
> Solomon was rich (1 Kings 3:5-14).

As John Phillips reminds us, the Old Testament rule equated godliness with prosperity.

But the New Testament blessing is quite different! Do you want to know what constitutes blessing? Read the Sermon on the Mount. It begins in Matthew 5 verse 3. God gives us no guarantee that He will give us health and wealth if we walk in His ways. We are God's heavenly people and our blessings are positional, spiritual and eternal (Ephesians 1:3).

John is saying:

"Gaius, you are weak physically but you are prospering spiritually. I long that your physical health would mirror your spiritual health."

That would be an interesting test to apply to us today!

If your physical health reflected your spiritual health, what would you look like?

Would some of you be in hospital? Would some of you be dead?

Would you be robust or weak? Strong or sickly?

Is your soul prospering?

"Art thou in health, my brother?" (2 Samuel 20:9)

(c) HIS EXCEPTIONAL TESTIMONY
Verses 3-4

"For I rejoiced greatly, when the brethren came and testified of the truth that is in thee, even as thou walkest in the truth. I have no greater joy than to hear that my children walk in truth."

Gaius was known as a man who obeyed the Word of God and *"walked in truth"*.

Was Gaius led to Christ through the apostle John? Or, was he a member or leader of an assembly under John's care? The word: *"my"* can be rendered: *"my own children"*. It does seem that John led Gaius to Christ - and what a joy that is! But it is an even greater joy to hear of Gaius growing in grace and standing up for the truth.

The false teachers who were knocking at the door of *"the elect lady"* in 2 John would receive short shrift at the door of Gaius. He would get the ugly truth of them in no time and send them away with a warning to steer clear of his flock.

But, more than that, Gaius was not only *standing for the truth* - he was *walking in the truth*. Gaius read the Word, meditated on it, delighted in it, and then practised it in his daily life. He was like the blessed man of Psalm 1 verse 3. His entire life was wrapped up in the truth. You see, true living comes from the living truth. The Lord Jesus, the truth (John 14:6), is revealed in the Word, which is God's truth (John 17:17). The Holy Spirit is also truth (1 John 5:6) and He teaches us truth.

The Spirit of God uses the Word of God to reveal the Son of God and then to enable us to obey the will of God and *"walk in truth"*.

What an exceptional testimony Gaius had! What about your testimony? Do other believers cringe when your name comes up because you have no testimony? John never had to fear when Gaius' name came up!

Is your appetite for divine things still good?
Do you rest in the Lord?
Are you walking in the truth?
Are you a dynamic Christian?

(d) HIS PRACTICAL MINISTRY
Verses 5-8

"Beloved, thou doest faithfully whatsoever thou doest to the brethren, and to strangers; Which have borne witness of thy charity before the church: whom if thou bring forward on their journey after a godly sort, thou shalt do well: Because that for His name's sake they went forth, taking nothing of the Gentiles. We therefore ought to receive such, that we might be fellowhelpers to the truth."

We have no indication that Gaius himself was a preacher or teacher, but:

1. He opened his Home to the Servants of God

We have learned from John's second letter the importance of Christian hospitality in that day. When the preachers and teachers were travelling from place to place, they did not have motels or hotels to stay in. There were inns but they were infested with fleas and known as places of immorality. Because of that, the believers opened up their homes to these travelling preachers.

Alexander Strauch says:

"If you doubt that hospitality was 'a distinctive mark of Christians and Christian communities', consider the following quotation: 'Indeed was there ever a visitor in your midst that did not approve your excellent and steadfast faith or did not proclaim the magnificent character of your hospitality'. These glowing words of praise concerning hospitality were written in A.D. 96 by the church in Rome to the Christians in Corinth."

I wonder: could these words concerning hospitality be said of us? How seriously have we taken the hospitality commands of the

227

New Testament? Is your home open to the servants of God, to the people of God? Is it not an indictment on us, that we are so reluctant to offer hospitality to the travelling preacher?

But not Gaius! This man, whose name means: *"down to earth"*, opened up his home to the servants of God. These travelling preachers were coming through to where John was and they would say: *"There is a man named Gaius in that church who extends Christian hospitality and he is such a blessing!"*

Do you practise hospitality? As an elder? (1 Timothy 3:2) As a deacon? As a believer? Peter says: *"Use hospitality one to another without grudging"* (1 Peter 4:9). Are our homes really at the disposal of Christ?

W.A. Criswell was one of the great Southern Baptist preachers. He says that it was through his parents' ministry of hospitality that he was saved. When he was 10 years of age, a preacher came to their town to hold an evangelistic campaign. His mother, Anna Criswell, invited him to stay with them.

The young W.A. Criswell was greatly impressed by the visiting evangelist, John Hicks. When the evangelist went out for a walk, little W.A. would walk with him. As he was going to and from the meetings, W.A. would go with him. When he was in the home during meals, he would sit close to the preacher and listen to the conversation. *John Hicks took time with that little boy, and by the time the evangelist left his home, W.A. Criswell had trusted the Saviour.*

By way of contrast, the story is told of the man who took his dog to the vet and asked him to cut off his tail completely.

The vet said:

"I am not sure I could do that. Why would you ever want me to do that to your dog?"

"Well", said the owner, *"my mother-in-law is coming to visit us and I don't want anything in the house to suggest she is welcome!"*

Is this not the way our hospitality often is? We do it reluctantly, not like Gaius who had an open home.

2. *He opened his Heart to the Servants of God*

In verse 6, the phrase: *"bring forward on their journey"* means: *"to assist on their journey"*. It meant more than giving them a friendly *"Good-bye"* or handshake. It included making adequate provision for the next step of the journey (1 Corinthians 16:6 and Titus 3:13). Here was a man who opened his home, his heart, his hand to the servants of God. *Practical Ministry to the servants of God!*

You may say: *"Why should we engage in this kind of ministry to the servants and people of God?"*

Well, John gives us the answer. He says:

(a) *It Glorifies the Lord*

John is dealing with the matter of supporting those who teach and preach the Word. He uses the phrase: *"after a godly sort"*. It means: *"worthy of God"* or: *"as befits God"*. We are never more Godlike than when we are sacrificing to serve others. Since these itinerant preachers were representing the name of the Lord, any ministry to them was really a service to Jesus Christ (Matthew 10:40 and Chapter 25:40).

(b) *It Testifies to the World*

God's servants do not derive their support from a lost world. God's people are responsible to support God's work. Verse 7 says: *"Taking nothing of the Gentiles"* or *"Receiving no help from the pagans"*.

Is this not a rebuke to those who beg from all, saint and sinner alike, to support their work? As if the Lord needed His work to be financed by the unsaved! When God's people adequately support God's servants, it is a powerful testimony to the lost. But, when pastors, missionaries and societies go about soliciting from the unsaved world, it makes the gospel look cheap and commercial.

(c) It Signifies our Obedience

Do you see what John says in verse 8? *"We therefore ought to show hospitality to such."* You see, this ministry of hospitality and support is not only an opportunity – it is an obligation.

Do you recall Paul's words to the Galatian believers?

He says:

"Let him that is taught in the Word communicate unto him that teacheth in all good things." (Galatians 6:6).

He is simply saying:

"Those who receive spiritual blessings through the ministry of the Word ought to share with the teacher of the Word material blessings" (1 Corinthians 9:7).

As Paul puts it in 1 Corinthians 9 verse 11: *"If we have sown unto you spiritual things, is it a great thing if we shall reap your carnal things?"*

(d) It Unifies the Church

When we *"receive"* God's servants and have a part in their ministry, we become *"fellow-helpers to the truth"* (verse 8). The word *"receive"* really means: *"to underwrite, to foot the bill"*.

Some of you in your heart of hearts would have liked to preach the gospel and some of you have dreamed about going to the mission field, but it did not work out. However, as you pray, give and help others you become a fellow-helper to the truth. You share in the ministry.

A story is told about William Carey, one of the best-known early missionaries. When Andrew Fuller said to him: *"There is a gold mine in India, but it seems almost as deep as the centre of the earth"*, Carey immediately replied: *"I will venture down, but remember you must hold the ropes"*.

Hosting or assisting the Lord's servants is one way we can *"receive"* or support or hold the ropes for those who venture out in His name.

It is one thing to fight apostasy and refuse to entertain false teachers – that is the message of 2 John, but it is another thing to open up our homes and our hearts and our hands to promote the truth. That is the message of 3 John.

Are you like Gaius? Is your ministry marked and motivated by love?

(2) In *DIOTREPHES*, we have a picture of CARNALITY
Verses 9-12

Do you recall that Paul identified some believers at Corinth as *"carnal"*? (1 Corinthians 3:1). W.E. Vine says that *"carnal"* means they were: *"governed by human nature instead of by the Spirit of God"* (1 Corinthians 3:3). *"Me, first, foremost and finally"* sums such a person up.

Who was Diotrephes? This name occurs everywhere in Greek literature. It is identified with Greek aristocracy, even nobility. Evidently this man was upper class, among the elite, when he came to know the Lord. He was accustomed to be in the limelight and that is where he wanted to stay. He was trying to run the church! He was the church boss.

Have you ever met such a person? Of course you have. A *"church boss"* might be an elder, a pastor, a deacon or even a layperson who has no official role in the church. Sometimes it can be a wealthy or influential person. But they feel that it is their job to run everything and everyone in the church.

J. Vernon McGee writes:

"There is generally one like him in every church who wants to control the church and the preacher. This man tried to be the first pope. He was Diotrephes the Dictator."

Do you see:

(a) HIS PERSONAL AMBITION
Verse 9

"I wrote unto the church: but Diotrephes, who loveth to have the preeminence among them, receiveth us not."

The word *"pre-eminence"* comes from two Greek words which mean: *"to be fond of being first"*. Here was a man who loved to be first. He runs on a: *"me first, look out for number one"* programme. Diotrephes had to be first in everything. Number one! He was running the show!

How often the work of Christ is hindered, the local church is stymied because some Diotrephes is so filled with pride, with himself, that he wants to be top dog all the time.

Dr. Lee Robertson, a Baptist in the U.S.A. and a noted Greek scholar, wrote an article about Diotrephes for a denominational publication. The editor of the magazine later rang him and told him that 25 officials from various churches had cancelled their subscription to show their resentment against getting personally attacked.

The sons of Diotrephes are still with us!

Did you know that there are only two places in the New Testament where the word *"pre-eminence"* occurs? Do you know where the other one is? Paul says in Colossians 1 verse 18 that Christ is the one who is supposed to have pre-eminence: *"That in all things He might have the pre-eminence"*.

You see, the bottom line is, it is either self or Christ. There are no big shots or little shots in this local church. Christ ought to be number one.

(b) HIS TOTAL ANTAGONISM
Verse 9

In verse 9, John says: *he "receiveth us not"*. In verse 10, he adds: *"neither doth he himself receive the brethren"*.

It would seem that John had written to the church but that the letter was intercepted and destroyed by this man Diotrephes. Is it not incredible to think Diotrephes, who may have been a church leader, intercepted John's letter, refused to have fellowship with one of the Lord's own apostles, and would not allow faithful preachers into the pulpit.

Why? Why did Diotrephes reject John? Because John challenged this man's right to be dictator in the church! John was a threat to Diotrephes because John had the authority of an apostle. John knew the truth about Diotrephes and was willing to make it known. Imagine Diotrephes refusing to acknowledge the leadership of John!

"Total antagonism." Does that describe your attitude to your spiritual leaders? You see, often when a member wants power, prestige and position, he usually attacks the leadership privately and publicly. Sometimes he starts a whispering campaign and tries to undermine the character and ministry of the leaders. Like Absalom in the Old Testament, he *"hints"* that the present leadership is not efficient (2 Samuel 15:1-4) but that if he were in power, he could handle things better.

Hebrews 13 verse 17 instructs us:

"Obey them that have the rule over you, and submit yourselves: for they watch for your souls, as they that must give account, that they may do it with joy, and not with grief: for that is unprofitable for you."

But, is the spirit of Diotrephes about you?

Do you notice:

(c) HIS VERBAL ACCUSATION

"Wherefore, if I come, I will remember his deeds which he doeth, prating against us with malicious words: and not content therewith, neither doth he himself receive the brethren, and forbiddeth them that would, and casteth them out of the church."

"Prating against us with malicious words" means: *"bringing false and empty charges against us"*. *"Prating"*, in Greek *"phlyareo"* means: *"to talk nonsense"*.

Is this not what Diotrephes was doing? What Diotrephes was saying about the apostle John was sheer nonsense, but there are people who love to hear such talk and they will believe it.

The church of the Twenty-first Century is no different from the church at the end of the First Century. There are gossips today. There are those who make false accusations against the servants of the Lord. That is why we need to be careful about everything we hear and read about the servants of God. If we could only remember that we are to listen to no accusations brought against the leadership of a work without witnesses present would that not solve the gossip problem? (1 Timothy 5:19).

Now, are you beginning to see Diotrephes in his true light? He wanted to be *"top dog"*. He would not receive John or the brethren. He was making false accusations.

He was also acting like a dictator, for look at:

(d) HIS DICTATORIAL ACTION

These Christians who received John's associates were dismissed from the church.

It seems that this man had enough power and enough of a following to excommunicate people who disagreed with him. He had neither the authority nor the Biblical basis for throwing these people out, but he did it.

The New Testament does teach church discipline (1 Corinthians 5:1). There must be rule in the church and there cannot be rule without rulers, but there is no place for the Diotrephes type. Do you recall Peter's words to the elders? *"Neither as being lords over God's heritage, but being ensamples to the flock"* (1 Peter 5:3).

An elder is not to be a dictator. Certainly, the elders have to rule, but they are to be examples to the flock. There must always be that balance between truth and grace.

Now when you stand back and look at Diotrephes' life, what do you have? A picture of carnality. Indeed, John in verse 11, with both men in mind, exhorts us to follow that which is good (Gaius) and avoid that which is evil (Diotrephes).

"Beloved, follow not that which is evil, but that which is good. He that doeth good is of God: but he that doeth evil hath not seen God."

(3) In *DEMETRIUS*, we have a picture of CONSISTENCY

Many scholars believe that Demetrius was the man who carried this brief letter to its destination. Moreover, Demetrius could encourage the heart of Gaius:

You could take the Word of God and put it next to the life of Demetrius - and he was consistent. His practice was in keeping with his profession. Says John: *"If you want to imitate an example, follow Gaius or Demetrius"*. The word *"follow"* in verse 11 means: *"to imitate or mimic"*.

Is it right for us to imitate human leaders? Yes, if they in turn are imitating Jesus Christ. Paul says: *"Be ye followers of me, even as I also am of Christ"* (1 Corinthians 11:1. See also Philippians 3:17). We cannot see God, but we can see God at work in the lives of His children. The godly life and dedicated service of another believer is always an encouragement and a stimulus to us (Hebrews 10:24). Demetrius was that kind of person.

Now who was Demetrius? Is he the same man mentioned in Acts 19? The silversmith of Ephesus and the leader of the opposition to Paul? (Acts 19:24) Did this Demetrius get saved? Did he then become a preacher of the gospel? One thing is sure, this Demetrius was marked by consistency. Look at his testimony.

(a) There was a UNIVERSAL Testimony

"Demetrius hath good report of all men, and of the truth itself: yea, and we also bear record; and ye know that our record is true" (verse 12).

"Demetrius hath good report of all men!" He was well spoken of by everyone. Not only believers but non-believers were impressed by his life. What a recommendation for the gospel when a follower of Christ impresses and attracts those around by the reality, consistency, and sincerity of his life!

Of course, when all men, saved and lost, good and evil, speak well of us, it may mean that we are compromising, but that was not the case here. Demetrius not only had a Universal Testimony, but also:

(b) There was a SCRIPTURAL Testimony

Demetrius was well spoken of by: *"the truth itself"*. What does that really mean? It simply means that our friend Demetrius was living his life in accord with the truth of Scripture. When his life was measured by that yardstick, the truth itself confirmed his quality.

He was like Gaius. He was walking in the truth. Is that what you are doing? Does your life harmonise with the teaching of Scripture?

(c) There was a PERSONAL Testimony

John says: *"Yea, and we also bear record"*. John knew firsthand that Demetrius was a man of God, and the apostle was not ashamed to confess it.

What kind of testimony do *you* have in your church fellowship? Do the believers know you and love you and thank God for your consistent life?
All of us, no doubt, have heard of *the Nobel Prize*. Do you know how it came about?

One morning in 1888, Alfred Nobel, who was the inventor of dynamite and a man who spent his life amassing a fortune from the sale and manufacture of weapons, read in the morning newspaper his own obituary. It was a simple journalistic error. Alfred's brother had died and a French reporter carelessly had got the wrong brother.

Alfred was shocked because he saw himself for the first time the way the rest of the world saw him. They called him: *"The Dynamite King"*, the great industrialist who made a fortune from explosives. As far as the public were concerned, the entire purpose of his life was to be a merchant of death.

That morning as he read down his own obituary with shocking horror, he resolved from that day on to make clear to the world the true meaning and purpose of his life. He decided to do it by disposing of his fortune when he died, and his will and testament would be the expression of his life's ideals.

The result was the most valued of prizes given to those today who have done most for the cause of world peace, ***the Nobel Peace Prize.***

Here is my challenge to you!

Imagine tomorrow morning your obituary suddenly appears in the paper. Would it say anything in any way related to God's work? Or would it be all about your own work, your own wealth, your own career, your own family? What would it say? When all is said and done, is this not what really matters? What will you be known for? What will you be remembered for?

Like Gaius, will you be remembered for your Charity?
Or, maybe like Diotrephes, will you be remembered for your Carnality?
Or, like Demetrius, will you be known for your Consistency?

Three men at the end of the First Century typical of three believers in any given local church in the Twenty-first Century.

Can I ask: Which one is you?

CHAPTER 26
Jude

Hugh Latimer (1487-1555) was a Fellow of Clare College, Cambridge and Bishop of Worcester before the Reformation. Later, he was the Church of England chaplain to King Edward VI. In 1555, under the Roman Catholic Queen Mary, he was burned at the stake. On 14th April 1554, commissioners from the Papacy began an examination of Latimer and two others - Nicholas Ridley and Thomas Cranmer. Latimer, hardly able to sustain a debate at his age, responded to the council in writing. He argued that the doctrines of the real presence of Christ in the Mass, transubstantiation, and the propitiatory merit of the mass were unbiblical. For holding these beliefs, Latimer was convicted of heresy and sentenced to death.

At length came the morning of 16th October 1555 when Latimer was led forth out of Oxford jail to die with his younger companion, Ridley.

Ridley embraced his friend. They knelt down and prayed together. Then after removing their outer clothes and giving little remembrances to their friends, they were ready for the fire. Mercifully, a friend hung a bag of gun powder round the neck of each of them, and then they were chained back to back to the post and the fire was brought.

"Play the man, Master Ridley", said Latimer. *"We shall this day light such a candle by God's grace in England as I trust shall never be put out."*

As the flames rose up, Hugh Latimer bathed his hands in them, as it were, until they reached the powder, and he died.

Why did Hugh Latimer die?

Because he was prepared to stand against an apostate system, the Roman Catholic Church! "Apostasy" comes from the Greek word *"apostasia"* and means: *"a falling away, a revolt or defection from the truth of God"*.

Dr. Alan Cairns says:

"The use of the word in Acts 21:21 (*"thou teachest all the Jews which are among the Gentiles to forsake Moses"***) shows that it properly describes a forsaking of the great truths of the Word of God."**

 S. Maxwell Coder writes:

"An apostate has received light but not life. He might have received, in some degree, the written Word but he has not received the living Word, the Son of God."

Clarence Sexton says:

"Apostasy is a subtle rejection of essentials while maintaining the outward form of belief."

The book of Jude is all about apostasy. It is the last book in the Bible but one. This fascinating little book has been called: *"the vestibule or the entrance hallway of the book of Revelation"*. So it is! It brings us into the waiting room of the Apocalypse and prepares us for the closing scenes in the drama of the end times.

Someone has said:

"The beginning of the age of the church is described in the Acts of the Apostles. The end of the church age is set forth in the Epistle of Jude, which might well be called – 'the Acts of the Apostates'."

Here is the only book in the New Testament which is devoted exclusively to apostasy, the abandonment of Biblical truth.

Now, what do we know about:

1. The Author of this Letter

Can you see his *Identity*?

Jude.

Jude is an English form of the Greek word: *"Judas"*, which translates the Hebrew name: *"Judah"*. This was a very common name. We find it quite often in the New Testament. Jude or Judas is a name that is now synonymous with betrayal for the disciple Judas – Judas Iscariot - was a traitor. He became the worst apostate the world has ever known and now, in the providence of God, this word ushers in a book that is devoted entirely to the subject of apostasy.

But who was this Judas? Well, says verse 1:

"Jude, the servant of Jesus Christ, and brother of James."

And who was James? He was a leader of the Jerusalem church (Acts 15:13); he was the man who wrote the epistle of James (James 1:1), and he was the half-brother of the Lord Jesus. So Jude was one of our Lord's half-brothers (Matthew 13:55 and Mark 6:3). They did not believe in Christ while He was ministering (John 7:5), but after the resurrection James was converted (1 Corinthians 15:7) and we have every reason to believe that Jude was also saved at that time (Acts 1:14).

Can you see his *Humility*?

"Jude, the servant of Jesus Christ." He is not standing on ceremony. Some people might have written: *"I am one of Jesus' half-brothers and the brother of James"*. But he was so down to earth. *"I am the brother of my brother and a slave of Jesus Christ."*

Can you see his *Company*?

As we study this little letter, we will discover that many verses in Jude parallel 2 Peter 2. Jude was written after Peter. Peter prophesied that false teachers would come (2 Peter 2:1 and Chapter 3:3). Jude says that they are now here and are at work.

2. The Audience of this Letter

The exact audience to whom Jude sent this letter is unknown. Possibly they were the same believers to whom Peter wrote (1 Peter 1:1). But one thing seems fairly certain. In light of Jude's illustrations, we can say that they seem to be Jewish converts.

Jude was writing to genuine believers. This is seen in the opening verse where he addresses his readers as:

"Sanctified by God the Father, and preserved in Jesus Christ, and called."

Other versions, following another early manuscript, translate the clause like this: *"called, beloved in God the Father and kept"*. There is an echo here of 1 Peter 1 verse 2 where all three Persons of the Godhead are seen to be involved in our salvation.

We are *"called"*.

We heard the call of God and we responded:

> *"I heard the voice of Jesus say,*
> *'Come unto Me and rest,*
> *Lay down, thou weary one, lay down,*
> *Thy head upon My breast'.*
> *I came to Jesus as I was,*
> *Weary and worn and sad,*
> *I found in Him a resting place*
> *And He has made me glad."*

We are *"loved"*. *"Beloved by God the Father"* or *"In God the Father"*.

The word indicates that God has placed His love on believers in eternity past (Ephesians 1:4-5) with results that continue in the present and into the future.

He loved me then, He loves me now and He will love me hereafter. There is nothing we can do to make God love us more than He loves us right now and there is nothing we can do to make Him love us any less.

But there is something else:

We are *"preserved"* or: *"kept for Jesus Christ"*.

These apostates would fall, sin and suffer condemnation, but true believers would be kept safe in Jesus Christ for all eternity.

Do you appreciate your position? Do you count your blessings? *"Called, loved and kept."*

In verse 2, Jude writes:

"Mercy unto you, and peace, and love, be multiplied."

Incidentally here is another triplet. Jude was very fond of them. As Sam Gordon remarks, maybe Jude was a preacher in his spare time and he loved a three point outline!

"Mercy, peace and love."

J. B. Hewitt says: *"Mercy is God for us, peace is God with us and love is God in us"*.

Now, do you see to whom Jude is writing? Perhaps to some particular church but in a broader sense to Christians everywhere.

Now what about:

3. The Aim of this Letter

S. Maxwell Coder observed:

"James wrote his epistle to inform us of the need and importance of good works and Jude wrote his letter to advise of the danger of evil works."

Do you see what Jude himself says in verse 3?

"Beloved, when I gave all diligence to write unto you of the common salvation, it was needful for me to write unto you, and exhort you that ye should earnestly contend for the faith which was once delivered unto the saints."

Jude had intended to write a very different sort of letter when the Holy Spirit directed him to write about apostasy. He wanted to take us to Calvary to tell us more about that *"so great salvation"* purchased for us with the precious blood of Christ. But, even as he begins to write, the Holy Spirit changes Jude's mind. As John Phillips says: *"Instead of a manuscript, we have a memo; instead of a theology, we have a thunderbolt"*,

Jude is writing this letter to condemn apostasy and to urge believers to contend for the faith.

The first section of the book tells us *why* to contend: because of false teachers.
The last section of the book tell us *how* to contend: showing our true resources.

This little book, written about 68-70 A.D. is a wake-up call to the church of Jesus Christ. This is a call to arms. This is Jude sounding the trumpet. This is truth for our times.

Now, the devil has tried to stop God's work two ways classically. One way is through **persecution.** Sometimes he does stop the church by persecution, but he does not succeed with real Christians. When real Christians are persecuted, when the devil tries to stamp out the fire, he just seems to scatter the embers and new churches start elsewhere.

The devil, therefore, tries another way. It seems to be more effective for him. Not persecution, but *infiltration*. He tries to infiltrate the church with error. Is this not one of the greatest threats to the church? Perhaps the greatest?

During external pressure, the church continues to thrive, but internal corruption is another thing! That is why Jude writes this epistle.

I have divided it into three parts:

(1) THE ATTACK
Verses 1-4

There is an attack from Apostasy!

Sound doctrine is under siege. In fact, it always has been. The attack on truth is as old as human history.

Do you recall how Satan in the Garden of Eden sought to distort God's Word?
Do you recall how he doubted God's Word? *"Yea, hath God said?"* (Genesis 3:1).
Then do you recall how he denied God's Word? *"Ye shall not surely die"* (Genesis 3:4).

Has this not been his tactic even since? No wonder the Lord Jesus called him: *"a liar, and the father of it"* (John 8:44).

Here was Jude's burden, his concern, his passion. He intended to write an explanation of the faith but need turned him to write an exhortation to defend the faith. Why? Because false teaching was infiltrating the church, seeking to lead many astray.

Have *we* forgotten the importance of truth? Have *we* failed to consider the repeated warnings in Scripture about apostasy?

Do you recall that the Lord Jesus in Matthew 24, in that great passage about the end times, said: *"Many false prophets shall rise, and shall deceive many"* (Matthew 24:11)?

In his farewell speech to the elders at Ephesus, recorded in Acts 20, Paul warned of this in verses 29 and 30:

"For I know this, that after my departing shall grievous wolves enter in among you, not sparing the flock. Also of your own selves shall men arise, speaking perverse things, to draw away disciples after them."

Paul cautioned Timothy:

"Now the Spirit speaketh expressly, that in the latter times some shall depart from the faith, giving heed to seducing spirits, and doctrines of devils" (1 Timothy 4:1).

Paul continued:

"If thou put the brethren in remembrance of these things, thou shalt be a good minister of Jesus Christ" (1 Timothy 4:6).

How would you define: *"a good minister"*? Well, Paul says he is one who alerts God's people to the danger of apostasy!

Peter in 2 Peter 2 verse 3 and John in 1 John 4 verses 1 to 3 and again in 2 John 7 also warned of the danger that false teachers posed to the church.

Why, John says:

"If there come any unto you, and bring not this doctrine, receive him not into your house, neither bid him God speed: for he that biddeth him God speed is partaker of his evil deeds" (2 John 10-11).

So, do you see here:

A Journey Through The Bible

(a) THE DANGER TO THE CHURCH
Verse 4

"For there are certain men crept in unawares, who were before of old ordained to this condemnation, ungodly men, turning the grace of our God into lasciviousness, and denying the only Lord God, and our Lord Jesus Christ."

Jude was disturbed because false teachers were attacking the church from within.

Look at their Presence

These false teachers were already present. The word *"unawares"* means: *"slipping in secretly with an evil intention"*. They had wormed their way into the congregation.

Did you ever see a clip of an alligator lying on the bank of a river then slithering into the water so subtly, secretly, and silently that he is unnoticed? Well, that is the picture here.

It is one thing to have false teachers outside the church who oppose the Word of God openly, but it is another thing to have counterfeit pastors, elders, deacons and members within the church who oppose the Word of God subtly.

Look at their Prophecy

"Who were before of old ordained to this condemnation."

This simply means that long ago God pronounced damnation against all apostates (Isaiah 8:20-22; Jeremiah 5:13-14 and Chapter 8:12-13).

Is this not what Enoch's prophecy – referred to later - was all about? Here was a man who at the beginning of history prophesied of the doom of apostates.

Look at their Practice

"Turning the grace of our God into lasciviousness."

"Lasciviousness" means: *"licentiousness"*. It means they told people that grace permitted them to live as they pleased. They felt that they had a licence to live an immoral, sexually degraded life. They simply said: *"The grace of God is so broad that the Lord will forgive you anything you do"* (Romans 6:1).

Do you ever hear that idea within society or even within the church? *"Sure! if I love someone, anything I do with that person is justified!"*

Christians are in danger of going astray if they think that as long as they are believers moral conduct does not matter - and that is what Jude is warning about.

Look at their Problem

"And denying the only Lord God, and our Lord Jesus Christ."

Jude is not writing about two different persons here.

As Warren Wiersbe says:

"The Greek construction demands that these two names refer to one Person."

In other words, Jude is declaring the *Deity* of our Lord Jesus Christ. Jesus Christ is God.

Now apostates all sooner or later attack the truth about Jesus Christ. Apostasy is an attack on His person or work.

But look at that statement again: *"Denying the only Lord God, and our Lord Jesus Christ."*

Do you see here the *Uniqueness* of our Lord Jesus Christ?

We live in a *"multi-religion"* country. The man in the street has decided that all religions are right. Many of them would say that they are *"favourable"* towards Jesus Christ, but the key word in this expression is *'only'*. Do you see it? *"The only Lord God, and our Lord Jesus Christ."* Do not be fooled by people who say: *"Oh yes! I believe in Jesus!"* but they do not believe in the Uniqueness of Christ. They do not believe that He is the only name whereby we must be saved.

Ask them:

"Do you believe He is the only way, not just a way? The only truth, not just a truth? The only life, not just a life?"

You will find they do not. They do not accept Christ as unique.

This was the danger to the church. Their *belief* was unscriptural and their *behaviour* was ungodly.

But do you see here:

(b) THE DUTY OF THE CHURCH
Verse 3

How are we as Christian believers to react to this danger? Well, look at verse 3:

"Beloved, when I gave all diligence to write unto you of the common salvation, it was needful for me to write unto you, and exhort you that ye should earnestly contend for the faith which was once delivered unto the saints."

I want you to notice here:

The FAITH

It is described later, in verse 20, as: *"your most holy faith"*. There is:

A Clearness about this Faith

Jude is not talking here about something which is subjective but about something which is objective. He is not talking about the act of believing but of: *"things which are most surely believed"* (Luke 1:1). You see, there is a vital distinction made in the New Testament between: *'faith'* and *'The Faith'*. Faith is the act of believing but the Faith is the sum total of revealed Truth. To put it simply, as Sam Gordon says: *'the faith is the Word of God'*.

A Comprehensiveness about this Faith

In this little letter, Jude mentions most of the fundamental articles of the Faith which we are to defend. For example, we have:

The Fact of sin – verse 4
The Doctrine of Grace - verse 4
The Glorious Person of Christ - verse 4
Eternal life through Christ - verse 21
The existence of a personal devil - verse 9
The Divine Trinity - verses 20-21
The Personality of the Holy Spirit - verses 19-20
The Sovereignty of God - verse 25
The Eternal Security of Believers - verse 24
The Fact of Judgment and Hell - verses 6, 7 & 13
The Divine Inspiration of the Scriptures as proved by its
prophetic and historical accuracy - verses 5-19
The Personal return of Christ - verse 14

Here then is *The Faith* as Jude defines it.

A Completeness about this Faith

"The faith which was once delivered unto the saints."

Once! The same Greek word (*"hapax"*) is used in Hebrews 9 verse 26 where we read: *"But now once in the end of the world hath He appeared to put away sin by the sacrifice of Himself"*.

Just as there is no more sacrifice needed for sin, so there is no more Scripture needed for the saint.

In every sense of the word, it is a finished work. It is complete. We have it all. Do you know what this means? It means we can rule out so-called prophets, prophecies and others forms of new revelation which the Charismatic Movement claim is still forthcoming. They say that the Bible is still being written. *"No!"* says Jude, *"The Bible is complete"* (Revelation 22:18). This is all the truth we need for every spiritual need in life.

The Faith but notice also:

The FIGHT

Do you see the phrase: *"earnestly contend"*? The Greek word gives us our English word: *"agonize"*. It is the picture of an athlete competing in the Greek Games and stretching his nerves and muscles to do his very best to win. You see, ***while the modernist contests the faith, the true believer must contend for the faith.*** It is a call to arms. It is a summons to battle. It is to put up a real fight. This vigorous defence of the faith must be done continually, conscientiously and compassionately. Matthew Henry says: *"earnestly but not furiously"*.

Are you not glad that the truth of God was not delivered to theologians or bishops but rather delivered to you? In so many churches today, the gospel is watered down, it is neutralized, it is compromised, and it is replaced. Think of the inroads the enemy has made in schools, Bible colleges, denominations, pulpits, on the radio, and television.

Why should we be silent when our precious faith is being attacked?
Why should we be sidelined when denominational leaders seek to undermine the Bible?

They attack the person and work of Jesus Christ and tell us that Hell is a figment of our imagination!

The great reformer, John Calvin, said this:

"Even a dog barks when his master is attacked. I would be a coward if I remained silent when God's truth is being attacked."

Let me ask you: Do you know anything about contending for the faith?

> Do you stand for the truth?
> Do you stand with the truth?
> Do you stand by the truth?

(2) THE ARGUMENT
Verses 5-15

About Apostasy

What a picture we have here of an apostate. You see, Jude traces the history of spiritual apostasy from before time to the end of time. In so doing he tells us that:

(a) False Teachers are Doomed
verses 5-7

Jude refers to three groups who apostatised.

Firstly, he refers to: **Unbelieving Israelites**

You will recall that the nation was brought out of Egypt by the power of God and was brought to the border of the Promised Land. But they did not have enough faith to go in and possess the Land (Numbers 13-14). The result? They wandered aimlessly for forty years and all in the camp twenty years and older died (Numbers 14:29). The entire nation was delivered but that does not mean that each individual was saved. A *"mixed multitude went up also with them"* (Exodus 12:38). They were *"fellow travelers"* who had joined the movement, but they missed the most important thing of all, the blood. These false disciples, like Jude's false disciples, were destroyed.

Secondly, Jude refers to: **Unsubmissive Angels**

Could it be that these were the angels who consorted with the daughters of men in Genesis 6 verses 1 to 4 and produced a race of giants? Whatever the details might be, the bottom line is, they rebelled against God and paid dearly for it.

Thirdly, Jude refers to: **Ungodly Cities**

Sodom and Gomorrah! These cities at the southern end of the Dead Sea had fallen into perverted sexual practices. Do you recall that when God's angels visited Lot's house, the men of the city surrounded Lot's house and ordered him to send his guests out to them so that they might indulge their lusts. God judged that city for its sin.

Someone has said:

"If God does not punish America, He will have to apologise to Sodom and Gomorrah."

What a day we live in when Protestant churches are ordaining men who indulge in the vile sins of Sodom.

One thing is sure. False teachers are doomed.

(b) False Teachers are Denounced
Verses 8-10

Do you see how Jude begins verse 8? *"Likewise also ..."* or: *"In the very same way"*. He is simply saying that history is repeating itself. As it was, so it is. This is what was happening in Jude's day and what about our day? Are we not back to the days Jude so vividly paints? People who are marked by sexual immorality (*"defile the flesh"*), by insubordination (*"despise dominion"*) and by slander (*"speak evil of dignities"*).

"Why", says Jude, *"even Michael did not treat the devil flippantly but said, 'The Lord rebuke thee'"*.

But Jude goes a step further:

(c) False Teachers are Displayed
Verse 11

Do you want to know how the apostate church thinks? Well, look at the men in verse 11:

"Woe unto them! for they have gone in the way of Cain, and ran greedily after the error of Balaam for reward, and perished in the gainsaying of Core."

"The way of Cain" is described in Genesis 4 verses 1 to 7. He brought a bloodless sacrifice to God. He denied the efficacy of the blood and the need for Calvary. Is this not the way of apostate liberals in our day? They look to culture instead of to Calvary. Is the way of Cain not with us today? It was William Booth, the founder of the Salvation Army, who said the chief danger facing the modern church was to proclaim: *"a religion without Christ, a salvation without regeneration, and a heaven without hell"*.

"The error of Balaam" involved leading others into sin for personal gain. Balaam knew the truth, but he deliberately led Israel into sin that he might make money. (Numbers 22-25) He was in it for what he could get out of it! Do we not need to be careful about our motives?

"The gainsaying of Core." Do you recall that Korah led a rebellion against Moses, the official spokesman for God? (Numbers 16:3) For this great sin, he was send down into the pit, the earth opening its bowels and swallowing him.

Harry Ironside said:

*"'The way of Cain' is **false religion**, 'the error of Balaam' is **false ministry**, and 'the gainsaying of Core' is **false worship and rebellion** against God's authority."*

A Journey Through The Bible

(d) False Teachers are Described
Verses 12-16

Jude gives us five word pictures of an apostate.

They are *Dangerous*

"These are spots in your feasts of charity, when they feast with you, feeding themselves without fear"

The word *'spots'* means: *'hidden rocks'*. They can sit with you at the Lord's Supper but they will bring your work to ruin.

They are *Deceptive*

"Clouds they are without water"

They are empty when it comes to fulfilling promises!

They are *Dead*

"Twice dead"

Twice dead, because they have only been born once!

They are *Disturbed*

"Raging waves of the sea"

Is this not how Isaiah described the godless in Isaiah 57 verses 20 and 21?

"But the wicked are like the troubled sea, when it cannot rest, whose waters cast up mire and dirt. There is no peace, saith my God, to the wicked."

They are *Doomed*

"Wandering stars, to whom is reserved the blackness of darkness for ever"

254

Indeed, Enoch right at the beginning of history prophesied of their doom. Should our hearts not be stirred when we think of loved ones who are going out into *"the blackness of darkness for ever"*?

(3) THE ANSWER
Verses 17-25

What is the answer to Apostasy? How are we to act in the light of this situation? How are we to defend the faith against apostasy? Well, notice we are to:

(a) ACCEPT THE WORD OF GOD
Verses 17-19

Look at verse 17:

"But, beloved, remember ye the words which were spoken before of the apostles of our Lord Jesus Christ."

Remember what? The words of the apostles. Men like Paul (1 Timothy 4:1-3); Peter (2 Peter 2:1) and John (1 John 4:1) said that false teaching would infiltrate the church. You see, one of the main tests of the Early Church was this: *Is this what the apostles taught?*

When the church assembled the New Testament books, it was required that each book be written by an apostle or by someone close to an apostle. Apostolic teaching was and still is the test of truth.

O. S. Hawkins reminds us:

"The truth is: if the words are new, they are not true."

What is our defence against apostasy? Our defence is what Jude calls *"your most holy faith"* (verse 20). We must know the Word of God and have the courage to defend it.

Sam Gordon, in his helpful book on Jude, quotes R.C. Sproul who says:

"We fail in our duty to study God's Word not so much because it is difficult to understand. Not so much because it is dull and boring. But because it is work. Our problem is not a lack of intelligence, or a lack of passion. Our problem is that we are lazy."

If you want to study God's Word, it will involve hard work. You will need to put your mind, your heart and your soul into it.

(b) APPROACH THE THRONE OF GOD
Verse 20

"Praying in the Holy Ghost."

What does it mean to pray in the Holy Spirit? It means to pray according to the leading of the Spirit.

We need a Spirit-energized prayer life. Praying in the Spirit. Not praying for the Spirit! As Christians, we already have the Spirit. The Spirit came to us at our conversion. So, not praying for the Spirit or for the gift of tongues.

This is Holy Ghost praying. Praying under the direction of the Holy Spirit. *Pleading the merit of the Saviour's blood and the pleading the promises of the Word of God.*

(c) ABIDE IN THE LOVE OF GOD
Verse 21

"Keep yourselves in the love of God."

Now, Jude did not say: *"Keep yourselves saved"* for he had already assured them that they were *"preserved in Jesus Christ"*. Rather, he wrote: *"Keep yourselves in the love of God"*.

Christ made a similar statement when He said: *"Continue ye in My love"* (John 15:9). It simply means that we must stay obedient to God. Is that not where blessing is promised? Do you recall what the Lord Jesus said? *"If ye keep My commandments, ye shall abide in My love"* (John 15:10).

But there is something else here:

(d) AWAIT THE SON OF GOD
Verse 21

"Looking for the mercy of our Lord Jesus Christ unto eternal life."

The word translated *'looking'* means: *"earnestly expecting"*. Is this your attitude as you await the return of the Lord Jesus?

(e) ADDRESS THE ENEMIES OF GOD
Verses 22-23

"And of some have compassion, making a difference: And others save with fear, pulling them out of the fire; hating even the garment spotted by the flesh."

Compassion is to be shown to those who have been led astray by false teachers. Do you see what Jude says? *"Making a difference."* In other words, treat each situation individually. It seems that there are three different groups here who need spiritual help.

Another translation puts these verses like this:

"And have mercy on some who are doubting, save others snatching them out of the fire, and on some have mercy with fear, hating even the garment polluted by the flesh."

In other words, we are to show pity to those who are in *Doubt* (the *Confused*); to those who are in *Danger* (the *Convinced*) and to those who are in *Definite Sin* (the *Committed*). All the time watching, that we are not defiled by them ourselves.

You see, no one is beyond the grace of God. Not even those who have fallen prey to false teachers. People can be saved. Do you believe that? Are we involved in the work of rescuing the perishing?

John Wesley said: *"You have only one business and that is the salvation of souls"*.

Here is the antidote to the poison of false teaching.

But there is something else here:

(f) ACKNOWLEDGE THE ABILITY OF GOD
Verse 24

"Now unto Him that is able to keep you from falling, and to present you faultless before the presence of His glory with exceeding joy."

In verse 1, we are kept *for* Jesus Christ. In verse 24, we are kept *by* Jesus Christ.

You see, despite all that the apostates say or do, we are eternally secure. One day the Bridegroom will present the Bride faultless in glory and what a day that will be!

Does that not encourage you to:

(g) ADORE THE PERSON OF GOD
Verse 25

"To the only wise God our Saviour, be glory and majesty, dominion and power, both now and ever. Amen."

Jude, whose name means: *"praise"*, closes this brief, brave book on the brightest note.

> **He is able:** the Power of God
> **To Keep:** the Preservation of God
> **And to Present:** the Purpose of God
> **Exceeding Joy:** the Pleasure of God

God will have pleasure in His own.

Jude is reminding us of the Greatness, the Grace, the Glory and the Government of our wonderful Saviour.

If only believers would see Him, they would never be led astray.

This is the God we worship.
This is the God we adore.
This is the God we serve.

This is the faith for which we contend.

May we say like Martin Luther:

"Here I stand. I can do no other. God help me!"

CHAPTER 27

Revelation

On one occasion, the *"Prince of Preachers"*, C.H. Spurgeon, was accosted by a critic with a question from the Bible:

"There now, can you tell me what that means?"

The man wanted to trip the preacher up!

With a twinkle in his eye, Spurgeon replied:

"Why, of course I can tell you what it means. It just means what it says."

That might well be an appropriate reply when people ask the question: *"What does the book of Revelation really mean?"*

Perhaps these words may apply here also:

"A question may be asked in a sentence - the reply may take a century."

One thing is sure - the book of Revelation is one of the most difficult to interpret, to comprehend and to explain. Perhaps one of the reasons for that is that Satan fights against us in our understanding of this book.

David Pawson says:

"The devil hates the first few pages of the Bible which reveal how he gained control of our planet and the last few pages which reveal how he will lose control of it. If he can convince humans that Genesis is composed of myths and Revelation of mysteries he is content."

Yet, no book in the Bible has an introduction and a conclusion quite like this one.

It commences with a promised blessing:

"Blessed is he that readeth, and they that hear the words of this prophecy, and keep those things which are written therein: for the time is at hand" (Revelation 1:3).

It closes with a promised blessing:

"Behold, I come quickly: blessed is he that keepeth the sayings of the prophecy of this book" (Revelation 22:7).

Admittedly, much of this book is difficult to understand, but just to hear the prophecies of this book being read is a blessing in a troubled world like ours.

Now, in order for us to understand this book at least in a little way, let me introduce it with five words:

1. ATMOSPHERE

What is the atmosphere or mood behind this book?

Well, John's own personal circumstances give us a clue. Do you see what he says in Chapter 1 verse 9?

"I John, who also am your brother, and companion in tribulation, and in the kingdom and patience of Jesus Christ, was in the isle that is called Patmos, for the word of God, and for the testimony of Jesus Christ."

John was exiled to Patmos towards the end of the First Century probably put there by Domitian, the Roman Emperor from 81 until 96 A.D. You see, it was Domitian who instigated emperor worship. Everyone who spoke to him had to address him as: *"Lord and God"*. Do you see now why John was labouring in the mines and quarries of Patmos? Busting rocks on a chain gang. This man would not surrender to any but his Lord, Jesus Christ.

So, throughout this book, we see the sufferings of God's people.

John is in exile – Revelation 1 verse 9.
The church in Smyrna will face imprisonment – Revelation 2 verse 10.
Antipas is martyred – Revelation 2 verse 13.

But, God is on His throne and working out His sovereign purpose.

2. APPROACH

How do we approach a book like Revelation?

Well, basically there have been four different approaches:

There is the Approach of *the Preterist*

The Latin word *'preter'* means: *'past'*. This interpretation states that everything in the book took place in the First Century. So, according to this view, John wrote to the saints to encourage them in their time of persecution. But, John states seven times (Revelation 1:3, Chapter 11:6, 19:10, 22:7, 10, 18 and 19) that he is writing *"prophecy"* (Greek word: *"propheteia"*). This is a book that deals with predictions. It deals with people and events which lie in the future.

There is the Approach of *the Historicist*

This view holds that the book has been in the process of being fulfilled throughout the whole Christian era.

Harold Willmington states:

"Those who hold this view see in the symbols the rise of papacy, the corruption of the church and the various wars throughout church history. Most of the reformers interpreted the book in this manner."

There is the Approach of *the Idealist*

They spiritualize the teaching of the Book. They tell us that it does not set forth actual events at all but that its symbols depict spiritual realities. But again, John tells us that he is writing prophecy dealing with events that one day will take place in the world.

There is the Approach of *the Futurist*

This approach emphasizes that Revelation is prophecy and that the major part of the book has to do with what is still future.

3. AUTHOR

Who is the author of the book of Revelation? Well, look at the first verse in the book:

"The Revelation of Jesus Christ, which God gave unto Him, to shew unto His servants things which must shortly come to pass; and He sent and signified it by His angel unto His servant John."

This book had its origin not in the mind of John but in the mind of God.

But, how did the Lord convey the contents of this book to His servant John?

The Father gave the revelation to the Son (Matthew 24:36) and the Son shared it with the apostle using *"His angel"* as intermediary. So here is John in Patmos, a penal colony of Rome, receiving this wonderful Revelation concerning end time events.

But what is the:

4. AIM

What is the purpose of this book? Well, look at its title. It is not the Revelation of St. John the Divine. It is the Revelation of Jesus Christ. It is all to do with **Unveiling**! The word *"revelation"* is from the Greek word *"apokalypsis"* which means: *"an uncovering, an unveiling or a disclosure"*. The central person of the book of Revelation is not John but Jesus Christ. So, if we study Revelation and do not learn anything about Christ, then we have misread the book. Revelation is meant to be an unveiling of Christ to us, but it also tells of the time when Christ's glory will be unveiled or revealed to all people. When Christ came to us the first time, His Glory was veiled, but when He comes again, His Glory will be completely unveiled.

Now, when studying Revelation, it is very easy to become focussed on trying to decipher and understand the prophecy. However, our main focus is to be on the One whose coming is prophesied. After all, it is not the Coming we want to be familiar with but the Person who is coming!

Imagine a train station. In that station, there is a station master whose main objective is to know as much as possible about all the trains. Thus he has all kinds of intricate charts to help him predict exactly where a train is and when it will reach the station. Now imagine that there is a young lady at the station. She is not nearly as well-informed as the station master, but she knows that her fiancée is on the train that is about to arrive, and she can hardly wait for him to get there.

Our hearts also need to beat in anticipation of the arrival of the King.

You may find a justification for your point of view or you may find reasons to support some fine point of prophecy, but if you do not see the Lord Jesus in the book of Revelation, you have missed the real point. This book is pre-eminently the revelation of Jesus Christ.

It is all to do with **Unfolding**. This book is essentially a book of prophecy. It shows us how all the events of human history have been pointing toward a single event, the return of Jesus Christ to establish His kingdom.

Unveiling; Unfolding; but also Upholding

We must not forget the practical import of this book. Remember it was written during a time of intense persecution, during the reign of that vicious Roman Emperor Domitian who declared himself to be lord and god of his people.

Where were these believers going to find encouragement?

Was there any hope for the future?
Is there any hope for the future?

Revelation answers these questions with a resounding: *"Yes!"*

God is still on the throne. All of history including their time of trouble and your time of trouble is under His control, the control of One who is coming again to defeat evil and establish His reign.

5. ANALYSIS

How can we analyse this book?

We may find it difficult because the scenes alternate between heaven and earth. For example, in Chapters 2 and 3, we are on earth as we consider the seven churches. But, in Chapters 4 and 5, we are in heaven to see the Lord Jesus step into the spotlight and receive the scroll, the title deed to earth. Then, in Chapter 6, we come back down to earth to see what happens when the seals are broken.

However, it can be analysed!

As far as I know, Revelation is the only book in the Bible that has an inspired outline. Do you see it in verse 19 of Chapter 1?

"Write the things which thou hast seen, and the things which are, and the things which shall be hereafter."

Here is the golden key to the book of Revelation.

It tells us that there is a Past, a Present and a Future in this book.

Here is the plan of the book:

"Things seen" - Chapter 1: His **Glory.**
"Things which are" – Chapters 2 and 3: His **Grace.**
"Things hereafter" – Chapters 4 to 22: His **Government.**

These three divisions are clear and they do not overlap. Each division is complete in itself and distinct from the other two. This is God's own division of the book.

(1) 'The Things Which Thou Hast Seen'
Chapter 1: The Past

The book of Revelation is a book of symbols and signs. Do you see verse 1 again?

"The Revelation of Jesus Christ, which God gave unto Him, to shew unto His servants things which must shortly come to pass; and He sent and signified it by His angel unto His servant John."

The word *'signified'* is interesting. If you want to get the true sense of the word, pronounce it aloud: *"SIGN-I-FIED"*. In other words, Christ made His revelation known to John by signs and symbols and once you grasp the symbolic *'sign-ificance'* of this book, you can understand it better. Here, in Chapter 1, we discover truth conveyed in the form of symbols. The Lord Jesus is described in a way that is not intended to convey His actual appearance but rather various aspects of His character, His attributes and His role. For example, what are the seven candlesticks and the seven stars? (Revelation 1:12, 16, 20) Well, the candlesticks are the churches and the stars are the angels.

It is clear from Chapters 2 and 3 that there is an angel assigned to each church. Some think that this refers to the leading elder. Vernon McGee writes:

"It is good to hear of pastors being called angels. Sometimes we are called other things!"

Observe here:

(a) THE AWESOME SIGHT
Chapter 1 verses 1-15

What a revelation of glory for an aged apostle! How thrilling it must have been for John who had witnessed the suffering of Christ now to see the glory of Christ. What compensation for an aged saint who was denied the usual privileges of the Lord's Day to get a vision of the Lord Himself.

Will you run your eye down this chapter and notice John's description of Christ? Do you see here:

The Humanity of the King: "One like unto the Son of Man" (verse 13). It was a full sixty years since John had last seen Jesus, but he immediately recognizes Him as "the Son of Man" (Daniel 7:13-14).

The Authority of the King: He was clothed with "a garment down to the foot" (verse 13). In ancient times, this was the recognised apparel of authority, dignity and rulership.

The Purity of the King: "His head and His hairs were white like wool, as white as snow" (verse 14). Is this not a symbol of Christ's absolute sinless holiness?

The Sagacity of the King: "And His eyes were as a flame of fire" (verse 14). Today we might say: "He has X-ray vision!" Christ cannot be deceived. He sees every minister, notes every member, observes every ministry and views every motive with X-ray vision.

The Severity of the King: "And His feet like unto fine brass" (verse 15). Brass in the Bible symbolises judgment. The Head of the church will judge sin in His churches.

The Integrity of the King: "And His voice as the sound of many waters" (verse 15).

The Sovereignty of the King: "And He had in His right hand seven stars" (verse 16). Christ is holding messengers in His right hand. It suggests His control of all things.

The Ferocity of the King: "*And out of His mouth went a sharp twoedged sword*" (verse 16). The sword is the Word of God (Ephesians 6:17 and Hebrews 4:12), and nothing can stand before it.

The Glory of the King: "*And His countenance was as the sun shineth in his strength*" (verse 16). Once that face was marred and spat upon: here it shines in resplendent glory (Matthew 17:2). It is that divine glory that John now beholds.

Do you think you have problems? The early Christians in general and John in particular faced tremendous problems. The believers were losing their homes, their livelihoods and in some cases their lives. But rather than focus on the problems, John:

> "Turned his eyes on Jesus,
> And looked full in His wonderful face,
> And the things of earth grew strangely dim,
> In the light of His glory and grace."

Sometimes when faced with great problems, our tendency is to focus on the **hands of God**! What He has not done for us and what we want Him to do for us - instead of focussing on the *face of God,* simply who He is.

Often, in the midst of great problems, we stop short of the real blessing God has for us, which is a fresh vision of who He is.

(b) THE ABJECT SERVANT
Chapter 1 verse 17

"*And when I saw Him, I fell at His feet as dead*" (verse 17).

Undone. Unmasked. Unravelled.

John caught one glimpse of the Holy One and his self-esteem was shattered.

Was it not the same for Isaiah? When he saw the sovereignty, purity, authority of the Lord Jesus, he cried: *"Woe is me! for I am undone"* (Isaiah 6:5 and John 12:41).

Was it not the same for Peter? When Peter realized he was standing in the presence of a Holy God, instantly he fell at Christ's feet: *"Depart from me; for I am sinful man, O Lord"* (Luke 5:8).

Is there not a dangerous absence of awe and worship in our churches? We are boasting about standing on our feet, instead of being broken and falling at His feet.

For years, Evan Roberts, the leader of the Welsh Revival at the beginning of the Twentieth Century, prayed: *"Bend me, bend me!"* and when God answered, the great Welsh Revival resulted.

But is it not the case that today there is - No fear, No awe, No reverence?

What we need is a true vision of Christ that will instil us with holy fear.

(c) THE ABSOLUTE SOVEREIGN
Chapter 1 verses 17-20

He Conveys His Sympathy: *"Fear not!"*

He Reveals His Identity: *"I am!"*

Why! did John not record seven of those sayings in his Gospel? Here is another one: *"I am the first and the last"*.

In the Old Testament, God said: *"I am the first, and I am the last; and beside Me there is no God"* (Isaiah 44:6 and Chapter 48:12).

By saying: *"I am the first"*, Christ lays claim to eternal pre-existence. By saying: *"I am the last"*, He is declaring that He is eternally immutable.

He says: *"I am He that liveth"*. That was another name that was applied to God (Joshua 3:10). He continues: *"Amen; and have the keys of hell and of death"*.

He Affirms His Authority

He is the All-Sufficient One: *"I am the first and the last"*
He is the All-Victorious One: *"I am He that liveth"*
He is the All-Powerful One: *"And have the keys"* Is this not encouraging? You see, despite cancer, growths, heart attacks and so on, you will never go through the door of death until He puts the key in and opens the door.

(2) 'The Things Which Are'
Chapters 2-3: The Present

Chapters 2 and 3 deal with the churches in this age of grace.

Now we can view these churches in a three-fold way. Firstly, we can view them:

(a) HISTORICALLY

First and foremost, these are seven letters written to seven actual, historical churches found in the Roman province of Asia, which was located on the western seaboard of what we now know as Turkey. Geographically, these seven cities form a rough circle and they are listed here in the order which a messenger might visit them. Sailing from the isle of Patmos he would arrive at Ephesus, he would then travel north to Smyrna and Pergamum, then south east to Thyatira, Sardis, Philadelphia and Laodicea.

The churches in this region were hard-pressed.

• *Circumstantially, there was Persecution*

The Emperor Domitian regarded himself as a *"God"*, so Christians who worshipped the Lord Christ were now being invited to worship the Lord Caesar. Once a year everyone in the Empire had to appear before the authorities and cry: *"Caesar is Lord!"*

What were the believers to do? They were faced with a choice - Caesar or Christ. To confess Caesar as Lord meant liberty, to confess Christ as Lord meant hostility, possibly death.

• *Doctrinally, there was Infiltration*

False prophets were abroad trying to deceive the churches into their heretical teachings (Revelation 2:2, 15 and 20).

• *Morally, there was Contamination*

Immoral men and women were contaminating the church by their influence. Standards of behaviour were being lowered (Revelation 2:14, 20).

So, the devil was attacking from several fronts.
Sometimes the onslaught was Physical, the Emperor.
Other times it was Doctrinal, false cults.
Still other times it was Moral, lowering standards.

Have the tactics of the devil changed? Are the same pressures not troubling our churches today? You might say: *"We are not being persecuted!"* Well, what about false cults? What about the continual desire to dilute the truth? What about the pressure of the world to conform the church to its own ways?

Do these seven letters not issue a call to endure persecution, to hold fast the truth, to obey the Lord?

(b) PROPHETICALLY

The plan of the book in Revelation 1 verse 19 seems to indicate this:
"The things which thou hast seen" - Chapter 1.
"The things which are" - Chapters 2 and 3
"The things which shall be hereafter" - Chapters 4 to 22.

So, Chapters 2 and 3 reveal to us conditions in the church from Pentecost to the Rapture. In other words, each church may be seen as representing a different phase in church history.

1. *Ephesus* (30-300). The name means: *"desirable"*. It represents the *Apostolic* Church. Even then a gradual cooling toward the Lord was evident.

2. *Smyrna* (100-313). The name means: *"myrrh"*. It represents the *Martyr* Church.

3. *Pergamos* (314-590). The name means: *"marriage"*. It represents the *Compromising* Church.

4. *Thyatira* (590-1517). The name means: *"continuing sacrifice"*. It represents the *Papal* Church.

5. *Sardis* (1517-1700) The name means: *"remnant"*. It represents the *Reformation* Church.

6. *Philadelphia* (1700-1900). The name means: *"brotherly love"*. It represents the *Revival* Church.

7. *Laodicea* (1900-Rapture). The name means: *"People's rights"*. It represents the *Worldly* Church.

So we may see in these seven churches, a panorama of prophecy from the day of Pentecost to the Rapture of the church.

Thirdly, we may view these seven churches:

(c) TYPICALLY

We might ask the question: *Why were there seven churches singled out by the Risen Lord?*

Certainly there were more than seven churches in this area (Acts 20:5, Colossians 1:2 and Chapter 4:13). Indeed, at the time the book of Revelation was written (95-100 A.D.), there may have existed over one hundred separate and independent local churches in the world. But out of the many, Christ chose seven typical churches and addressed Himself to these. Why?

Well, it seems that the spiritual conditions found in these seven churches are typical and representative of what every local church has been throughout her history and what she is like today.

Any condition of any church in any place at any time may be found here.

It may be that each of us will see our church depicted here in these letters. Do you know something? Every thoughtful believer will find himself mirrored here!

As we read the letters and see the state of each church, we will be confronted with a series of questions.

Are you an *Ephesian* believer? Have you grown cold in your love for the Lord?

Perhaps you are like the Christians in *Smyrna*. Are you suffering for Christ's sake?

Are you like those in *Pergamos*? Are you compromising the truth?

Are the believers at *Thyatira* a picture of you? Do you know what they believed in? Peaceful coexistence. One foot in the world and one foot in the Lord's camp.

Maybe you are like those in *Sardis*. Have you a reputation but there is no reality?

Like those in *Philadelphia*, could the Risen Lord commend you for your faithfulness?

Or, like the believers in *Laodicea*, are you lukewarm and is Christ about to spew you out of His mouth?

In these two chapters, the Risen Lord speaks His mind to His churches. It is in these chapters and not in Matthew 28 or Acts 1 that the final words of Christ to the church are recorded.

That means that Christ's message to these churches has a timeless relevance.

Indeed, if you look closely at these letters you will see the character of a New Testament church. What ought to be found within a New Testament church?

Love: The letter to Ephesus:
Suffering: The letter to Smyrna
Truth: The letter to Pergamos
Holiness: The letter to Thyatira
Reality: The letter to Sardis
Opportunity: The letter to Philadelphia
Wholeheartedness: The letter to Laodicea

(3) 'The Things Which Shall Be Hereafter'
Chapters 4-22: The Future

"Things seen" - Chapter 1: *His Glory.*
"Things which are" - Chapters 2-3: *His Grace.*
"Things hereafter" – Chapters 4-22: *His Government.*

Do you see the phrase: *"the things which shall be hereafter"* (*"meta tauta"*). The meaning is: *"Write the things which shall be after the churches, when the churches are no more"*. Now look at Chapter 4 verse 1:

"After this I looked, and, behold, a door was opened in heaven: and the first voice which I heard was as it were of a trumpet talking with me; which said, Come up hither, and I will shew thee things which must be hereafter."

So, Chapter 4 introduces the third section of the book.

Remember that Chapters 2 and 3 deal with seven successive

periods of church history which closes with the Laodicean age, which is the church of today. But note how Chapter 4 opens: *"After this"*. After what? After the church age. So from Chapter 4 through to Chapter 22 we have the third section of the book. It focuses on prophecy after the church age.

People have asked: *"Where does the Rapture come in?"*
It is in the white spaces between Chapter 3 and Chapter 4.

Look at that first verse again. What does that remind you of? It should remind us of both 1 Corinthians 15 verse 52 and 1 Thessalonians 4 verse 16. They tell us that there is going to be a trumpet blown when the Lord comes. One of these days, the Lord is going to say to the saints: *"Come up hither!"* What we have in this first verse is a picture of all believers being *"caught up"* to the throne at the Rapture.

The Rapture is the very first event in God's prophetic calendar – and John is summoned to Heaven. Why? Because God wants to show John:

(a) THE RULE OF THE LORD
Chapters 4-5

God wants to show John worldly events from a heavenly perspective. *Now, what exactly did John see?* John sees a throne, God's throne, sat in heaven.

John finds himself in the control centre for the entire universe. The central object of this headquarters is the throne of God.

Revelation is a throne book, the word being used some *forty five times.*
This is a throne chapter, for the throne is mentioned *thirteen times* here.

You ask: *"What is this all about?"*
Just this: Though the storm is over for the child of God, another is about to break loose on the earth. God's great government is

about to work itself out on the earth. The stage is now set, the church has been taken to Heaven, the Lord is on the throne, all of Heaven praises Him and awaits the outpouring of His wrath.

A challenge is thrown out to all humanity? *Who of all God's creatures is fit to rule the world? Who has the right to the title deed of the earth?*

The scroll in Chapter 5 is the title deed to the earth. In this book are the final end-time, cataclysmic judgments of God that will be poured upon the earth during the tribulation. The One who possesses this book and can break its seals possesses the right to rule the world.

The question posed was not: **"Who is willing?"** but: **"Who is worthy?"** (Revelation 5:2)

No one in Washington has the answers. No one in Moscow. No one in London. No one can execute God's plans for human history. We are hopeless and helpless to usher in the Golden Age. No wonder John wept! Is there anyone who can open the book? Is there anyone who can loose the seals? Is there anyone who can rule the world?

Bless God, there is One, Only One, the blessed Jesus, He's the One!

Christ is about to open the sealed book and release judgment on the world. You see, this is:

(b) THE RETRIBUTION OF THE LORD
Chapter 6 verse 1 to Chapter 19 verse 10

The Bible uses different titles for this blood-chilling period. It is called: *"The Day of the Lord"* (Isaiah 13:9); *"The Indignation"* (Isaiah 26:20); *"The Time of Jacob's Trouble"* (Jeremiah 30:7); *"The Seventieth Week"* (Daniel 9:27) and *"The Tribulation"* (Matthew 24:21).

Jeremiah spoke of this time:

"Wherefore do I see every man with his hands on his loins, as a woman

in travail, and all faces turned into paleness? Alas! for that day is great, so that none is like it: it is even the time of Jacob's trouble" (Jeremiah 30:6-7).

Joel spoke of this time:

"The day of the Lord cometh, for it is nigh at hand; a day of darkness and of gloominess, a day of clouds and of thick darkness" (Joel 2:1-2).

The Lord Jesus had this to say about this time:

"For then shall be great tribulation, such as was not since the beginning of this world to this time, no, nor ever shall be" (Matthew 24:21).

That is a remarkable statement! Considering all the wars, famines, heartaches, atrocities that have taken place on earth, to hear Christ say there is a time coming, the like of which the earth has never seen, makes one tremble.

According to Daniel 9, seven years are assigned to Israel in God's prophetic calendar.

It starts with the signing of a contract with the Antichrist and ends with Christ's return to earth to establish His kingdom.

It is this period that is described in Revelation 6 to 19.

Some scholars feel that the inspired outline in Chapter 1 verse 19 divides this period into three parts:
In Chapters 6 to 9, we have the first three and a half years.
In Chapters 10 to 14, we have the middle of the period when Antichrist breaks his covenant with Israel and becomes their persecutor instead of their protector.
Then in Chapters 15 to 19, we have the last three and a half years.

This seven-year *"week"* is characterised by three series of events.

(1) *The Seven Seals* – Chapter 6 verse 1 to Chapter 8 verse 5.

(2) *The Seven Trumpets* - Chapter 8 verse 6 to Chapter 11 verse 19.
(3) *The Seven Vials* - Chapter 16 verse 1 to Chapter 19 verse 21.

Can you picture the scene? The Lord Jesus is about to take back creation from the usurper Satan. But, as the Lord Jesus begins to break the seals in that scroll, so the judgments begin here on earth.

The Seals are broken, the Trumpets are sounded and the Vials are outpoured.

Each series of judgments, in an ascending scale of severity, flows from the other and each has its ultimate cause in the taking of the scroll by the Lord Jesus into His capable and pierced hands. Everything that now happens in the book of Revelation happens because He precipitates the action. From start to finish He is in complete control. Judgment is about to fall. Why? To punish the nations for their sin (Matthew 25:31-36) and especially the way they have treated Israel. Also, to purge Israel and prepare a believing remnant to receive Christ when He comes in glory.

This is:

(c) THE RETURN OF THE LORD
Chapter 19 verses 11-21

"And I saw heaven opened, and behold a white horse; and He that sat upon him was called Faithful and True, and in righteousness He doth judge and make war. His eyes were as a flame of fire, and on His head were many crowns; and He had a name written, that no man knew, but He Himself. And He was clothed with a vesture dipped in blood: and His name is called The Word of God" (verses 11-13).

This is none other than the Lord Jesus. He is coming in power and great glory.

Keep in mind that the Second Coming of the Lord Jesus will take in two stages.

At the Rapture, Christ comes to the air - 1 Thessalonians 4 verse 17.

At the Second Advent, Christ comes to the earth - Zechariah 14 verse 4.

Scripturally speaking the: *"Come up hither"* in Chapter 4 verse 1 is the Rapture, but the appearance of the White Horse Rider and his armies in Chapter 19 verse 11 is the Revelation of the Lord Jesus.

You see, *marriage imagery and martial imagery do not fit into the same picture.*
In the Rapture, the picture is that of a wedding: in the Revelation, the picture is that of a war.

The King is coming!

He is coming **Visibly:** *"Every eye shall see Him"* (Revelation 1:7).
He is coming **Victoriously.**
He is coming in **Vengeance.**

Look at Chapter 19 verses 19 and 20:

"And I saw the beast, and the kings of the earth, and their armies, gathered together to make war against Him that sat on the horse, and against His army. And the beast was taken, and with him the false prophet that wrought miracles before him, with which he deceived them that had received the mark of the beast, and them that worshipped his image. These both were cast alive into a lake of fire burning with brimstone."

This is the long looked for conflict of Armageddon. What a scene! West against East and East against West – and all against God. The armies of this world marching across the Plains of Esdraelon. Napoleon called this plain: *"The greatest battle field in the world".* The shipping fleets of the world at anchor in the Persian Gulf and along the shores of the Eastern Mediterranean. The aircraft of the world, darkening the skies above. Then, suddenly, it will all be over!

There will be just one word from Him who sits astride the great white horse. One word - and the war is over. The beast and the false

A Journey Through The Bible

prophet are bundled up and hurled headlong into the everlasting flames. The panic-stricken armies fall down dead. The vultures descend and cover the scene. Christ is victorious!

I heard the story of some theological students who were tired and confused by some lectures they were getting on the book of Revelation. So, they decided to go to down to the gym for a game of basketball. While they were playing they noticed their African-American caretaker reading his Bible while waiting to lock up. They asked which part he was studying and they were surprised to find that he was going through Revelation.

"You don't understand that do you?" they asked.

"Sure do!" he replied.

"What's it about then?"

With eyes lit up and a big broad smile came this reply:

"Simple! Jesus wins."

The old caretaker was right. This is the message of Revelation. Jesus wins.

And then the long awaited reign of Christ begins.

Do you see here:

(d) THE REIGN OF THE LORD
Chapter 20 verses 1-21

Look at that little phrase at the end of verse 4: *"And they lived and reigned with Christ a thousand years"*.

Bible scholars refer to this as the: *"Millennium"*, a Latin word that comes from the words: *"mille"* which means: *"thousand"* and: *"annum"* which means: *"year"*.

Think of it! Only a few hundred yards from where He wore a Crown of Thorns, He will wear the Crown of Glory. For a thousand years our blessed Lord will literally reign on this earth. Those who deny this literal reign are stripping the Lord of this coming glory!

At last we will be able to sing truthfully:

> *"Joy to the world the Lord is come,*
> *Let earth receive her King,*
> *Let every heart prepare Him room,*
> *And heaven and nature sing.*
>
> *No more let sins and sorrows grow,*
> *Nor thorns infest the ground,*
> *He comes to make His blessings flow,*
> *Far as the curse is found.*
>
> *He rules the world with truth and grace,*
> *And makes the nations prove,*
> *The glories of His righteousness,*
> *And wonders of His love."*

What a contrast this will be to the judgment, known as the Great White Throne judgment (Revelation 20:11-15) when sinners will come face to face with the Christ they rejected and: *"Whosoever was not found written in the book of life was cast into the lake of fire"* (verse 15).

Would that not stir you to reach the lost? To care for the dying? To tell them of: *"Jesus, the mighty to save"*?

Would you not like others to dwell in:

(e) THE RESIDENCE OF THE LORD
Chapters 21-22

Speaking of the eternal state, John says:

"Behold, the tabernacle of God is with men, and He will dwell with them,

and they shall be His people, and God Himself shall be with them and be their God" (Revelation 21:3).

The word: *"tabernacle"* (*"skene"*) literally means: *"the place where God dwells"*. Today, God does not live in man-made temples (Acts 7:48-50) but in the bodies of His people and in the church (1 Corinthians 6:19 and Ephesians 2:21). But, in the eternal state God will move into this city and live with all believers in intimate, continuous fellowship.

"I beseech Thee", says Moses. *"Show me Thy glory"* (Exodus 33:18). *"O God"*, says the Psalmist. *"Early will I seek Thee ... to see Thy power and Thy glory"* (Psalm 63:1-2).

Heaven will be peopled with millions of bright presences but all eyes will be fastened on and fascinated by the King in His beauty.

Frederick Faber penned the lines:

> *"My God, how wonderful Thou art,*
> *Thy majesty, how bright;*
> *How beautiful Thy mercy seat*
> *In depths of burning light!*
>
> *How dread are Thine eternal years,*
> *O everlasting Lord,*
> *By prostrate spirits day and night*
> *Incessantly adored!*
>
> *How beautiful, how beautiful,*
> *The sight of Thee must be,*
> *Thine endless wisdom, boundless power,*
> *And awful purity!*
>
> *O how I fear Thee, living One,*
> *With deepest, tenderest fears,*
> *And worship Thee with trembling hope,*
> *And penitential tears!*

Yet I may love Thee too, O Lord,
Almighty as Thou art;
For Thou hast stooped to ask of me
The love of my poor heart.

Oh then this worse than worthless heart
In pity deign to take,
And make it love Thee, for Thyself
And for Thy glory's sake.

No earthly father loves like Thee,
No mother, e'er so mild,
Bears and forbears as Thou hast done,
With me, Thy sinful child.

Only to sit and think of God,
Oh, what a joy it is!
To think the thought, to breathe the name,
Earth has no higher bliss.

Father of Jesus, love's reward!
What rapture it will be,
Prostrate before Thy throne to lie,
And gaze and gaze on Thee!"

Now we see Him by faith, one day we shall see Him by sight: *"And they shall see His face"* (Revelation 22:4).

We are going to see the Lord Jesus visibly, actually, literally, bodily – and what a moment that will be!

Do you see how this book of prophecy closes? Three times Christ says: *"Behold, I come quickly"* (Revelation 22:7, 12 and 20. The word: *"quickly"* (*"tachy"*) means: *"immediately, rapidly, imminently, swiftly"*. In other words, His coming is very, very soon. He is already on His way. He is ready to burst upon the scene of human history right now.

The book closes: *"John, tell people not to change one word of this Revelation"* (Revelation 22:18-19).

When you add to the Scriptures – that is Romanism.
When you take from the Scriptures – that is Modernism.

A curse rests on anyone who adds to or takes from the Word of God.

And then: *"John, I am coming soon"*.

Can you see this aged servant clapping his hands and saying:

"Even so, come, Lord Jesus."

Thus ends the last book of the Bible, the book of the last things.

Thank you for joining me on: ***"A Journey Through The Bible"***.

Surely we can end this *'journey'* in no better way than to echo this prayer:

"Even so, come, Lord Jesus."

> *"I am waiting for the coming,*
> *Of the Lord who died for me;*
> *Oh, His words have thrilled my spirit,*
> *'I will come again for thee'.*
> *I can almost hear His footfall,*
> *On the threshold of the door,*
> *And my heart, my heart is longing,*
> *To be with Him evermore."*

Also available by Denis Lyle:

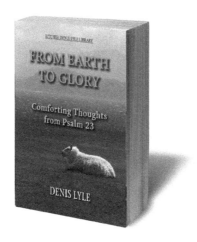

From Earth to Glory - Psalm 23
9781872734484

Available from:
www.ritchiechristianmedia.co.uk

Also available by Denis Lyle:

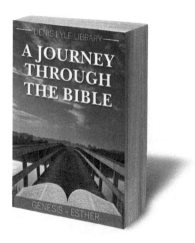

A Journey Through the Bible (Volume 1) - Genesis to Esther
9781872734552

Available from:
www.ritchiechristianmedia.co.uk

Also available by Denis Lyle:

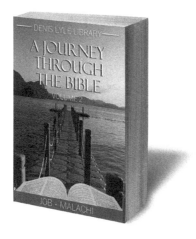

A Journey Through the Bible (Volume 2) - Job to Malachi
9781912522378

Available from:
www.ritchiechristianmedia.co.uk

Also available by Denis Lyle:

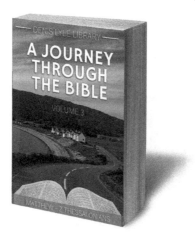

A Journey Through the Bible (Volume 3) - Matthew to 2 Thessalonians
9781912522637

Available from:
www.ritchiechristianmedia.co.uk